OCLC
WorldCat®

Advanced Search   Find a Library

Add to list   Add tags   Write a review   Rate this item: ☆☆☆☆☆

Linguistics manifesto : universal language & the super unified linguistic theory

Author:	Tienzen Gong
Publisher:	Diamond Bar, Calif. : PreBabel Institute, ©2010.
Edition/Format:	Print book : English
Database:	WorldCat

Find a copy in the library

Enter your location: 91745   [Find libraries]

Library

1. 🏛 **University of Illinois at Urbana Champaign**
   Urbana, IL 61801 United States

2. 🏛 **University of Wisconsin - Madison, General Library System**
   Madison, WI 53706 United States

3. 🏛 **University of Chicago Library**
   Chicago, IL 60637 United States

4. 🏛 **Georgia State University**
   Atlanta, GA 30303 United States

5. 🏛 **Cornell University Library**
   Ithaca, NY 14853 United States

6. 🏛 **Columbia University in the City of New York**
   Columbia University Libraries
   New York, NY 10027 United States

7. 🏛 **Brown University**
   Brown University Library
   Providence, RI 02912 United States

8. 🏛 **HCL Technical Services**
   Harvard College Library
   Cambridge, MA 02139 United States

« First ‹ Prev 1 2 Next › Last »

Truth, Faith, and Life

—I understand; Therefore, I worship—

Jeh-Tween Gong

ADAMS PRESS
CHICAGO, ILLINOIS

Library of Congress Catalog Card
Number 90-092907

International Standard Book Number
ISBN 0-916713-04-0

PRINTED IN THE UNITED STATES OF AMERICA

Preface

When I was in third grade, a debate about religion among a few of my classmates lasted for a few months. There were three major opinions, Buddhism, Christianity, and atheism.

My grandfather, father of my mother, was a bishop of Lutheran church. I was baptized in a Lutheran church when I was six years old.

I simply didn't understand why there are some atheists. It only costed me one penny a week to go to church then. If there were a God, I was glad that I bought a ticket for going to heaven. If there were no God, a penny a week was a very small loss. Besides, I had a lot of fun in church, singing songs and making friends.

When I was fourteen, I began to study the special relativity theory. I simply couldn't accept the interpretation of relativity by all scientists, as there is nothing absolute, regardless of how many scientific evidences exist. A higher truth must exist above all those scientific evidences. In fact, the interpreted conclusion of special relativity is the single most obvious self-evident evidence that science is unable to reach the domain of the utmost truth.

Science emphasizes proofs and experiments, which are both domain- and instrument-bonded. Therefore, the traditional science is unable to reach the utmost truth that is immutable. Religions emphasize the growth of faith but lack a solid methodology to demonstrate the validity of a faith. In the other words, science is unable to reach the region of infinity whose existence is very much self-evident all over the places. By the same token, religion is also unable to reach the region of infinity in the sense of a true understanding. Faith without understanding is hypocrisy, is superstition. Hobbes wrote, "Fear of a power invisible, feigned by the mind or imagained from tales publicly allowed is religion; not allowed, superstition."

For Hobbes, the criterion for a true faith is the principle of "conviction in common." But the principle of "conviction in common" is also the origin for reasoning. The acceptance of axioms and principles in mathematics and science is also the result of the principle of "conviction in common."

At age twenty-nine, in 1979, I was finally convinced that religions, science, metaphysics, and dialectic must be the different views of the same truth, and indeed they are.

This book is the summary of my conviction. There is one and only one God; therefore, one and only one utmost truth. Every being, every thing and every law flow out from Him. Furthermore, the Almighty God is self-evident and understandable. I understand; therefore, I worship. This book is trying to help you to attain this same understanding.

I do, however, not write for those who do not want to understand but carry their faith around for showing off and perfectly satisfy with the falsity they have got, nor for those who have no ability to understand because of their closed mind, nor for those who worship scientific methodology instead of the Almighty God.

Jeh-Tween Gong

Bristol, Virginia
December 25, 1989

Contents

PREFACE.. iii

CHAPTER

1   Book of Truth (I) — Empty truth, Limited truth, and
the Utmost truth 1

2   Book of Faith (I) — God, Paradoxicalness, and
Religions. 9

3   Book of Life (I) — What is Life? 17

4   Book of Truth (II) — Conservation laws, The creation
before the first creation, and the Ghost Partner 23

5   Book of Life (II) — Dimensions, Colors, and Unilogy 35

6   Book of Truth (III) — Forces, Building blocks, and
Colors.. 41

7   Book of Truth (IV) — Numbers, Colors, and Infinities ... 47

8   Book of Life (III) — Soul, Eternity, and Colors 57

9   Book of Life (IV) — Diversification, Freedom, and
Civilization 67

10   Book of Truth (V) — Chaos, the tomb stone of science.. 73

11   Book of Faith (II) — Confucianism, Taoism, and
Buddhism 83

12   Book of Faith (III) — Christianity 97

13   Book of God — God and His manifestations 107

14   Book of Ethics—Ten Commandments..........................117

15   Book of Truth (VI)—Super Unification.......................129

Empty truth, Limited truth, and the Utmost truth

We all hunger for truths, an urging hunger. But, what is the truth, why, what, and how? Who knows the truth? How can you prove you know the truth? How can you prove you know more than I do?

It is very stupid of many creationists to deny the evolution theory that is undisputable in its own domain, an era after the first creation. It is equally stupid of many scientists to deny the first creation event that is beyond the domain of the traditional sciences.

You are absolutely certain that your mother gave birth to start your life. You are equally certain that your grandmother gave birth to start your mother's life. But, your confidence will quickly diminish when you travel backward to the past trying to find out your roots. Who was the first creator? Where did he come from? If the first creator was created by someone else, then he cannot be the first creator, but this someone else is. It doesn't matter what title we gave to this "someone else," God, Lord, or Heavenly Father; this someone else is the first creator. Now, we are in a paradoxical (circular) trap. Nobody can create the first creator. So, the "nobody," is the first creator. The only way to come out of this trap is for the first creator to create himself. And, it simply doesn't make sense. But, who gives the "sense" the authority to judge what right or wrong is?

II

There are two fundamental methods for finding out an answer for a given question.

The first method is by evaluating many possible answers against known logic, evidences, and common sense. The foundation of this method is by denying any preference to a particular answer. All

1

possible answers are treated without discrimination at the beginning by the answer seeker. The selection process for selecting an answer is done mainly by evaluating the external evidences without any intervention by the preference of the answer seeker. But, it is very difficult to separate the answer and the mind of the answer seeker completely. Therefore, all answers that are found with this method are always subject to future challenges. It means that none of the answers is an absolute truth, but it is only the best answer we know today. Very often, a better answer can manifest out from nowhere tomorrow. This method of finding an answer for a given question is called SCIENCE.

III

The second method for finding an answer to a given question is by selecting an answer through FAITH. If an answer seeker believes in a particular answer, then his question has been answered. His quest to find an answer for his question has been completed. There is no reason for him to bother his already peaceful mind by evaluating any other possible answers. He found his answer, and he felt very good about it. He will often become very angry if anyone disagrees with his answer. It is not only an insult to his wisdom, but also disturbs his peaceful mind. But, this process of finding answers through faith does not work very well for some easy questions that already have a widely recognized answer. If anyone chooses to believe an answer that differs from this commonly accepted knowledge, he will often be viewed as ignorant, stupid, and uneducated. But, finding answers through faith does work for those questions that do not have a commonly accepted answer, such as the question of who God is. This type of answer obtains its authority through a disciplinary system — if you believe in this answer, then you will go to heaven; otherwise, you will be condemned and sent to hell. This method of finding an answer for a given question is called RELIGION.

IV

According to some religious doctrines, you do have the freedom of choice to choose your destiny. Do we have the right to determine whether "the truth" is right or wrong? If a "truth" can be judged by an external subject, then it is not an absolute truth. The absolute truth possesses its true value by itself, and no external force is able to change it. There is absolutely no such thing as the freedom of choice in the arena where the truth presides. We are either smart enough to recognize the true value of the truth or stupid enough to deny it, and both outcomes are the results of human beings' ignorance that should not be labeled as the freedom of choice. There is one and only one God, and that is that. We can do absolutely nothing about it.

During the past 2000 years, two groups of people have worked very hard side by side trying to find an answer for the question of whom the first creator was and where he came from by utilizing these two distinctive methods metioned above.

One group developed religions with FAITH. The religions not only are ways of belief, but they are cultures. A culture can only be built with life, millions of lives. A culture can survive without knowing true answers for many of the questions. Sometimes, two contradictory answers for the same question can evolve into two different cultures that are equally vivid, colorful, and long lasting. Amazingly, two contradictory assumptions can also often evolve into two distinctive but both correct sciences. The Euclidean geometry and non-Euclidean geometry are indeed evolved from two contradictory assumptions. Therefore, finding answers through faith is not a wrong thing to do. On the contrary, many cultures and civilizations have been developed through this process. Faith is not only good for religions but also for sciences.

Religions are part of human beings' lives. It is not only an important part of the believer's lives, but it is also an equally important part of the unbelievers' lives. The unbelievers are the persons who choose an answer that differs from the believers' answer. Nonetheless, the unbelievers also obtain their answer through their faith of unbelieving, not from any proven knowledge. So, religions are good. Religions are nice. Really, religions are necessary for comforting our minds and souls. But, do religions know the TRUTH?

The second group developed science. Scientists try to find an answer to a given question by not "giving" an answer. They want the answer to show its face by itself. Often, they ask a different question that may be an easier question to answer. Instead of trying to find an answer for the question of whom the first creator is, they often ask a new question such as: "Does the above question possess an answer?" If they can prove that there is no answer for the above question, then the question is answered, and the quest of finding an answer for the question has been completed. If they can prove that there is at least one answer existing, then it will be worth the effort to look for it. If they can prove that there are at least two answers existing for that question, then they will not stop looking after the first answer is found. Furthermore, scientists have invented a truth machine, and it works like this.

First, they select an answer any which way they prefer. Then, they put it through the front part of the truth machine that is called THEORY. This first part of the truth machine should spill out more material than it received. These spilled out materials are called predictions.

Finally, they put these predictions through the second part of the truth machine that is called LABORATORY. If those predicitons come out undisturbed, then the theory is correct and the assumption of the theory is also "assumed" to be correct.

There are two paradoxes in this process.

First, no one is able to put the creation process of the universe through a laboratory. If anyone could do it, then there is a chance that a new universe could be created in addition to our already existing one, and what kind of new world it would be. I deeply "BELIEVE" that some natural processes cannot be tested in any kind of laboratory. So, the chance for traditional science to find the utmost truth of how the universe and lives were created is very remote. Some changes for their old methodologies are necessary.

Second, very often, many predictions are true but their assumptions are found to be not true. How can a theory predict many correct predictions when it is developed and based on many false assumptions? These are true miracles. The fact is that many of those false assumptions have no direct logical connection with their predictions. Many such examples exist in the history of science. I will show you a few of this kind of examples in the later chapters.

God created the universe, stars, sun, earth, and lives. But, scientists created cars, air planes, and many good things for lives. So, science is good. Science is nice. Really, science is necessary for comforting our lives. But, does science know the TRUTH?

V

Does the truth exist? Or, what is the truth? What are we looking for?

The above questions can be grouped into three subjects.

1) What are truths — types of truth?
2) What are the sources of truths?
3) What are the criteria for truths?

There are three kinds of truth: empty truth, limited truth, and the utmost truth. Some truths are more true than others.

The first type of truth is empty truth.

"Where are you from?" asked a stranger. "From the place I came," I answered. "Come on! Daddy, be serious, tell him the truth," demanded Jason and Henry, my sons. "I did tell the truth, nothing but the truth," cried I.

Indeed, I told the stranger the truth, a useless truth for his question, an empty truth. We can find this kind of truth in many religious doctrines.

"And God said, Let there be light: and there was light." Genesis 1:3.

Nonetheless, the empty truth is not false nor always useless. On the contrary, many empty truths are quite useful not only for religions but also for sciences. Many sciences are based on one or a few empty truths. In mathematics, n factorial is defined as n times (n-1) factorial. This is a best example of reiterative definition, that a term is defined by itself. Maybe, the statement such as "I am I" does not always make sense, but many reiterative definitions are often the foundation of many sciences. God is precisely defined as "I am I" in Bible.

"And Moses said unto God, Behold, when I come unto the children of Israel, and shall say unto them, The God of your fathers hath sent me unto you; and they shall say to me, What is his name? what shall I say unto them? And God said unto Moses, I AM THAT I AM: and he said, Thus shalt thou say unto the children of Israel, I AM hath sent me unto you." Exodus 3:13-14.

The empty truth is a fuzzy picture of a truth. It is often meaningless in many aspects, but it is a truth nonetheless. Often, an empty truth becomes a meaningful truth when a culture is built upon it. Empty truth is frequently believer- and culture-bonded. It seems always true if you believe it. There are many different religions, and each of them is able to comfort their believers' minds and souls.

The criterion for all empty truths is faith. But, what a man believes cannot always be true. An idiot can often not know any truth. Furthermore, a man who speaks truthfully may in fact say what is false. Freud argued, "If it were really a matter of indifference what we believed, then we might just as well build our bridges of cardboard as of stone, or inject a tenth of a gramme of morphia into a patient instead of a hundredth, or take tear-gas as a narcotic instead of ether." In summary, what men believe cannot be the criterion even for the empty truth, although faith is indeed a very important part of the truth. In fact, the utmost truth can never be reached without faith. But faith alone can neither reach the utmost truth nor guarantee the validity of an empty truth. See Book of Truth (II).

The second type of truth is limited truth. This kind of truth is true only if it resides in its own domain. It is domain-bonded. There are many disciplines or branches of knowledge, and most of them are true only in their own domain. All known sciences, physics, chemistry, mathematics, are limited truths. This kind of truth can often be proved by some external evidences. But who gives these external evidences the supreme power of authority to do the judgment? The sources of all limited truths are experiences. All experiences and external evidences are time- and space-bonded. The criteria of these truths are the principle of contradiction, logic consistency and clarity. The principle of contradiction does not work beyond space- and time-domain, neither do all reasonings nor logic. Plotinus wrote, "The object known must be identical with the knowing act — If this identity does not exist, neither does truth — Truth cannot apply to something conflicting with itself; what it affirms it must also be." The criterion of truth from Plotinus is valid only for domain-bonded truth, a limited truth. Obviously, all domain-bonded truths are not the utmost truth.

The third type of truth is the utmost truth. This truth cannot be proved by any external evidences that are space- and time-bonded. This truth cannot be denied by simply not believing it. It is true regardless of whether anyone believes it or not. It is true regardless of whether time and space exist or not. This truth is eternal. This truth is immutable. The source of this truth is a "Self." Aquinas wrote, "Divine truth has no source — God Himself, Who is the primal truth — is the rule of all truth and the principle and source of all truth." The criterion for this truth is also the "Self." He can be neither proved nor disproved by either the principle of contradiction or reasoning which are both domain-bonded. Spinoza said, "— because truth is its own standard — or what can be clearer more certain than a true idea as the standard of truth? Just as light reveals both itself and the darkness, so truth is the standard of itself and of the false." This is the truth of God, how God was created! I will discuss this utmost truth in the Books of Truth.

The logic in this book is new but self-consistent. I have pointed out where God comes from and what God is with an understandable logic. I also have pointed out the needs of worshipping God although the mask of God has been removed. We all, all religions and all sciences, are permanently confined in God.

Book of Faith (I)
God, Paradoxicalness, and Religions

If the civilization was not born by religions, it is certainly brought up by religions. Science is a relatively young creature comparing with the human existence. Many great questions entered our ancestors' mind long before the birth of science, and many of these questions remain to be unanswered by traditional science.

There are many paradoxical logics still puzzling scientists today. For example, the statement of that "our universe is expanding outward" is a paradoxical statement. The definition of "universe" is "a whole body of things and phenomena." By definition, nothing can be outside the universe. How can our universe expand outward when there is no such thing as outside the universe? But, it is a scientific fact that our universe is expanding.

Actually, the foundation of all religions is the paradoxicalness. The common foundation of all religions is the question of who created the "first" creator. Most of the religions answer this great question with the answer of self creation hypothesis, but none of them provides an understandable mechanism of how it actually works. I have described a "nothing" — "something" transformation, which is a self creation process, and this is the first that a divine subject is introduced into science [See Book of Truth (II)].

II

Every religion lacks tolerance for any other religions. Each religion insists that its doctrine is the sacred Scripture, a divine revelation that has an absolute authority cannot be challenged or questioned by the human mind. This absolute truth, often contradictory, can only be revealed with faith, which is a Godsend gift. Therefore, the man with a different faith is surely an outcast, not by any man but by God. Thus this man must be evil and should be treated as enemy. There is no common ground among religions. Arguments among religions or between religion and science are absolutely useless, a waste of time. Surprisingly, after an in-depth study, all religions are constructed with identical architecture but with only different kinds of exterior decorations. Four corner stones are in common for all religions.

III

First, each religion recognizes a God in its own way. For some, the God has multiple images, such as gods and demigods in Buddhism. For others, there is one and only one God. But, this kind of difference is actually not significant. The truth is that there is one and only one God, but God manifests into eleven dimensions [See Book of Life (II) and Book of Life (III)]. There is one and only one unified force, but it diversifies into four fundamental forces. The important point here is the recognition of the existence of God regardless of which image is recognized.

There is one God, and it is a universal accepted concept. In Christianity, Jehovah created the whole universe in six days. In Taoism, this universe was created from "nothing." In Confucianism, this universe was evolved from a unitary Being who incarnates into two sexes, Mother earth and Father heaven. In Buddhism, this universe was created from "emptiness" [See Book of Faith (II)]. Unfortunately, this common sense is rejected by science. But, fortunately, science is still a small part of the civilization; its domain remains mainly in the material world. The social order and the spiritual inspiration are still the major forces for human civilization.

IV

The second corner stone is a logical consequence of the first one. Each religion developed a method to "connect" the earth lives with the supreme God. The concept of "connection" is also a common idea for all religions. But, the method of "connection" and "attainment" is different for every religion. This difference is the major difference between religions.

We do not have the freedom of choice to decide whether God exists or not because the existence of God is absolute. The way of our recognition of the existence of God will not effect the absolute existence of God one bit. We, human beings, are the beneficiaries by worshipping God. God gains nothing from us but He gives us comfort, confidence, and a peaceful mind if we submit ourselves to Him.

We do have the freedom of choice to choose the method of the connection. As soon as we have recognized the existence of God and have submitted ourselves to Him, the method of connection will not make much difference. Every religion is able to comfort its follower's mind. But, the method of attainment does influence the path of development of a culture significantly.

There are many different ways of connection, but most of them can be classified into two categories. One group chooses the method of "offering" to communicate with God. Judaism sacrifices a life as the offering:

"And he shall kill the bullock before the LORD: and the priests, Aaron's sons, shall bring the blood, and sprinkle the blood round about upon the altar that is by the door of the tabernacle of the congregation." Leviticus 1:5.

The practice of human sacrifice has never been recorded in the Bible, but the notion of using human sacrifice as offering to God does exist in the Old Testament:

"And they came to the place which God had told him of; and Abraham built an altar there, and laid the wood in order, and bound Isaac his son, and laid him on the altar upon the wood. And Abraham stretched forth his hand, and took the knife to slay his son." Genesis 22:9-10.

After the crucifixion, the blood of a perfect lamb is no longer good enough to offer to God by Christians. In Christianity, Jesus Christ is the Son of God, and His blood is the only connection between earth life and God:

"And ye know that he was manifested to take away our sins; and in him is no sin." 1 John 3:5.

The other group chooses the method of "meditation" and "enlightenment" to communicate with God by reaching the heavenly

state of "nothingness" or "emptiness." Taoism and Buddhism belong
to this group [See Book of Faith (II)].

Not only the ways of connection are different among religions
theoretically, but also the methods of attainment. In Christianity,
the attainment is through accepting the salvation of Jesus Christ:
"But if we walk in the light, as he is in the light, we have
fellowship one with another, and the blood of Jesus Christ his Son
cleanseth us from all sin." 1 John 1:7.
Most of the Christians do not believe that human "work" can
attain the salvation while the "work" is the only factor that will
be used on the judgement day:
"And I saw the dead, small and great, stand before God; and
the books were opened: and another book was opened, which is
the book of life: and the dead were judged out of those things which
were written in the books, according to their works." Revelation 20:12.
In Buddhism and Brahmanism, the salvation can only be attained
through work or many life-times of work to acquire the divine
knowledge and enlightenment:
"Gradually, step by step, with full conviction, one should become
situated in trance by means of intelligence, and this the mind should
be fixed on the self alone and should think of nothing else. From
whatever and wherever the mind wanders due to its flickering and
unsteady nature, one must certainly withdraw it and bring it back
under the control of the self. Steady in the self, being freed from
all material contamination, then it achieves the highest perfection
stage of happiness in touch with the Supreme Consciousness."
(Bhagavad-Gita as it is.)
Furthermore, the earth life is not the only entity that has to
be connected to God. All religions believe that there are souls for
lives. It is even more important to connect the souls to God. Surprisingly, all religions used a similar concept to make this connection,
and it is called heaven. All religions believe that the soul remains
alive after the death of the material body. All religions believe that
heaven is the place where souls and God meet face to face. It is
amazing how much similarity among religions does exist.
But, the meanings of heaven are different among religions. In
general, there are three interpretations.
First, heaven is a place where God resides. In the Bible, there
are three kinds of description of this place. Heaven is outside of

the earth. Heaven is the city of Jerusalem. And, heaven is a place for eternal life.

Second, heaven is a "state." In Buddhism, it is Nirvana, and it is a state of the extinction of the suffering and the annihilation of desire. This state is a state of "emptiness." The true nature of the universe is emptiness. The universe is created from emptiness, and God resides in emptiness. God is emptiness. To reach the state of emptiness is to unite with God.

Third, Heaven is a Self, and He is a different manifestation of God Himself, and all souls are resting in Him. God and Heaven is one entity. The universe is created from Heaven. Heaven is an infinity, and all souls converge into Him. This description is not only the best, but it is the utmost truth.

V

The third corner stone is that all religions believe in miracles as the divine confirmations. In the Old Testament, no Jew was able to perform miracles. All miracles were performed by God through the hands of His prophets. But, in the New Testament, Jesus was able to perform miracles by Himself. Even His disciples or followers are also able to perform miracles in His name. In Buddhism and Taoism, miracles can be performed only by Saints (Arhats or true man) who have attained deliverance.

Most religions also believe in reincarnation but with different interpretations. In Buddhism and Brahmanism, the reincarnation is a suffering, and the goal of these religions is to be freed from rebirth:

"While contemplating the objects of the senses, a person develops attachment for them. From such attachment comes lust, then anger, illusion, bewilderment of memory and loss of intelligence, and then one falls down into the material cycle of birth and death." (Bhagavad-Gita as it is.)

In Christianity, the reincarnation (born again) means salvation: "For the LORD himself shall descend from heaven with a shout with the voice of the archangel, and with the trumpet of God: and the dead in Christ shall rise first." Thessalonians 4:16.

VI

The fourth corner stone is the earth life. All religions are trying to connect earth life with the eternal life. The method of how to attain this connection becomes the ethical codes of earth life. The different views of the method of connection and attainment have developed into many different cultures.

In Christianity, the connection is through Jesus Christ; the attainment is by accepting Jesus Christ through fellowship:

"For by one Spirit are we all baptized into one body, whether we be Jews or Gentiles, whether we be bond or free; and have been all make to drink into one Spirit." 1 Corinthians 12:13.

"And whether one member suffer, all the members suffer with it; or one member be honoured, all the members rejoice with it." 1 Corinthians 12:26.

In reality, nobody is able to claim that he is a Christian if he is not a member of a church. The faith of believing in Christ can only be recognized by others through a membership of a church. To unify all members into one Body makes Christianity to become a super organism; therefore, the Western culture has much more energy than other cultures.

In Confucianism, the connection is through family ancestors. The barriers between families have never been broken. In Buddhism, the enlightenment can only be attained by the works of the individual himself. Therefore, the cultures that are influenced by these religions have no united goal and mission, and the energy of these cultures is much less than that of the Christian culture.

VII

In summary, all religions have to discuss four common subjects.

First, the existence of the Creator — Jehovah (Judaism), Krsna (Brahmanism), Shang-Ti (Confucianism), etc.

Second, a method of "connection" — through Jesus Christ, through acquiring the divine knowledge and enlightenment, through the Son of heaven, and through the ancestry worship. All these different ways of connection are using two common concepts, souls and heaven. But, the true connection is through one very important concept, which is the concept of "Self" [See Book of Truth (IV)]. The soul is a self. God is also a Self. The concept of "Self" does not exist in Christianity but does exist in Buddhism, Brahmanism, and Taoism.

Third, miracles — the manifestation of the power of God.

Fourth, the meanings and disciplines of the earth life — ethical codes, worship codes, and church codes.

The paradoxicalness is the fundamental part of the truth. God is unobservable. God is an infinity [See Book of Truth (IV)]. Our universe was born by a big bang that was an infinity, infinite density and infinite high temperature. Each scientific logic is valid only after the infinite-finite transformation was completed. All scientific logic is only a domain-bonded truth, a limited truth. A new truth machine has to be invented [See Book of Truth (II)].

From this view point, religions did a much better job than sciences did. The recognition of the existence of God is coming from the recognition of the limited ability of human being. After we have realized that we are able to beg for help from a super being, human beings have obtained unlimited confidence. Many of our ancestors undertook many enormous tasks, such as the great wall of China, the pyramids of Egypt, and many great cathedrals in Europe. All of these ancient achievements were results mainly from the religious faith and self confidence. The technical know-how was not the source of these achievements but a result of them. So, our civilization is the result of religious faith, and the self confidence is induced from our religious faith.

VIII

Basically, there are two types of religion, one with faith, the other with enlightenment. But, what is faith?

Locke wrote, "The highest degree of our assent upon bare testimony, whether the thing proposed agree or disagree with common experience, and the ordinary course of things, or no. The reason whereof is, because the testimony is of such a one as cannot deceive, nor be deceived, and that is of God Himself. This carries with it an assurance beyond doubt, evidence beyond exception. This is called by a peculiar name, revelation; and our assent to it, faith: which as absolutely determines our minds, and as perfectly excludes all wavering, as our knowledge itself; and we may as well doubt of our own being, as we can whether any revelation from God be true. So that faith is a settled and sure principle of assent and assurance, and leaves no manner of room for doubt or hesitation. Only we must be sure that it be a divine revelation, and that we understand [how?] it right."

Clearly, even with faith, men still need an "understanding" of the validity of the bare testimony and the divine revelation. Why are there so many different religions? How can a human mind distinguish which bare testimony and which divine revelation are true? What is the process to build up a faith?

Aquinas wrote, "Thus, in the science of geometry, the conclusions are what is known materially, while the formal aspect of the science consists in the means of demonstration, through which the conclusions are known. Accordingly, if in faith we consider the formal aspect of the object, it is nothing else than the First Truth [what is that?]. For the faith of which we are speaking does not assent to anything, except because it is revealed by God.

"The first is, to hold the truth of Scripture without wavering. The second is that since Holy Scripture can be explained in a multiplicity of senses, one should adhere to a particular explanation only in such measure as to be ready to abandon it, if it be proved with certainty to be false; lest Holy Scripture be exposed to the ridicule of unbelievers, and obstacles be placed to their believing."

Both Locke and Aquinas wasted much of their time in writing those meaningless words. Do you know what the origin of faith is now, in a true sense of understanding, not from your faith? Even though the content of Holy Writ can be the nutrition for the growth of faith, but the human mind itself has yet first to accept the Holy Writ is indeed the revealed truth of God. Faith without understanding is hypocirsy, is superstition. But, only faith can reach the domain that is much beyond the grasp of the traditional science. Faith is a Godsend gift, and it is the third principle of the new truth machine that is described in Book of Truth (II). I understand; therefore, I worship.

Book of Life (I)

What is life?

"And God said, Let the earth bring forth the living creature after his kind, cattle, and creeping thing, and beast of the earth after his kind: and it was so." Genesis 1:24.

"I am the original fragrance of the earth, and I am the light in fire. I am the life of all that lives, and I am the penances of all ascetics." (Bhagavad-gita as it is)

These statements do not provide a detailed procedure for how lives were created, but these answers are as good as any traditional sciences can provide.

Evolution science has constructed an undisputable process of how species evolve after the first mother was created, but the evolution theory is unable to explain or describe where the first creator came from. It is very stupid of many creationists to deny the evolution theory that is undisputable in its own domain, an era after the first creation. It is equally stupid of many scientists to deny the first creation event that is beyond the domain of their traditional sciences.

The stories in the Bible are actually better answers than any traditional scientific explanation concerning the question of the creation of the first mother. The Bible, however, does not provide an answer for where God came from. Actually, the question of where God came from has no meaning in Bible, and there is no reason to provide an answer for it. I, however, will provide an answer for the question of where God came from. But, at this point, I will discuss what lives are first.

II

There are millions of different kind of species existing on earth today. Some of them are very primitive, but some of them are highly

developed. How can we define what lives are? Can we find a definition that is capable of satisfying both disciplines of religion and
science? The answer is yes. And, from the answer of what lives
are, we are able to find the answer of where lives came from. We
are, however, unable to define what life is in one word or one
sentence. Seven and only seven characteristics are needed to describe
what life is for all lives.

1) All known life forms occupy space. The smallest virus can
only be seen under electron microscope, but it occupies space
nonetheless. On the other hand, occupying space alone does not
give an object a life. For example, a gold statue does occupy space,
but its existence has completely different meaning from what life is.

2) All life forms travel with time. Traveling with time is a
very important phenomenon in physics. When a particle stays
absolutely still in a fixed position in space, it is not still at all but
moving along with time. The moving time gives all particles a very
important gift that is called "mass." If any particle is trying to travel
faster than be still at a fixed point in space — having a relative
motion — then its mass will increase, and time will slow down for
it (this is the relativity theory). Time is the source of mass for all
material, and it is the source of gravitational force. All material
is time-borne, and there is aboslutely no way of getting off this
time train. Actually, time, space and mass are as trinity. Time
creates mass, and mass occupies space. All lives are time-borne, but
not all time-borne materials have life.

3) All lives are forms of material flow. In common language,
there are three types of material flow to sustain human life. If food
flow were cut off, a life would die in a few months. If water flow
were cut off, a life would be stopped in a few weeks. If air flow
were cut off, a life would be terminated in a few minutes. A virus
has no vital sign when it is outside of a living cell because there
is no material available for the virus to generate a material flow,
and it will become lively when it enters a living cell, which has
much of material needed for the virus to create a material flow.
However, material flow itself is not a life. The material flow only
represents a force, such as water flowing over a waterfall; or electrons flowing through power lines. Life is a living "force" but with
something more than just a force. I breathe, I eat, I am alive.

4) All species reproduce their own kind. This is the key
characteristic for separating the life forms from lifeless material.
Living lives are trapped in space and time, but all lifeless material

is, too. Some materials flow through a certain point or a volume of space. Some of them become the fuel of a machine that creates a mechanical force, and some of them become the fuel of a life, which creates a living force. Space, time and material flow are important parts of all lives, but many other lifeless things, such as machines, also possess these three characteristics. One of the major factors of separating life forms from lifeless things is the ability of life species to reproduce their own kind. With today's technology, it is possible to make a robot to reproduce itself. But, the difference between this pseudo-robotics reproduction and the reproduction of life is great. The robotics reproduction is driven by an external force, and it does not have a "desire" for reproduction. The reproduction of life is driven by an internal force, a "desire" of reproducing. Traditional sciences ignore many important facts and truths simply because of their own ignorance of being unable to define those facts clearly. The desire for reproduction is a very important fact for all lives. I reproduce; therefore, I am. This is the first hallmark for separating the life forms from lifeless material. For many creatures, the meaning of life is to reproduce; the goal of life is to reproduce. Many creatures end their lives after mating, such as salmon fish, preying mantis, and the male black widow spider. The end of one life is often the beginning of many new lives. The death of one salmon fish is not a failure but a triumph, not an end but a new beginning, not a waste but a successful mission.

5) All lives have intelligence. It is very obvious that all animals with a brain have some observable intelligence. For all brainless plants, their ingenuities are also evident everywhere. It is amazing how many different ways that plants employ to attract a third party to perform the task of sexual intercourse for them. This kind of plant, animals, and insect relationship is not a random event. Many plants and animals have a mutual bounding life line. Many plants produce nectar and fruits to award the animals and insects, which have helped plants to perform the intercourse between them. This designed relationship is often initiated by plants and is surely a result of the plants' intelligence. Even a single cell bacterium has intelligence. It can often change its surface chemical structure to fool attacking enemies. Even a virus that is only a naked DNA is often able to become immune from many toxic chemicals, which were fatal for the virus at the beginning. The ability to interact with the environment is the second hallmark for separating life forms from lifeless material. Someone may say that the ability to interact with the

environment is caused by a genetic mutation process. Yes, the genetic mutation process is the beginning of the intelligence. The invention of a bisexual reproduction method has further speeded up the growth of intelligence for lives [see Book of Life (III)].

6) All lives have feelings. Again, it is very obvious that all animals have some observable feelings and emotions. Even some plants have some observable feelings or senses. Artists are the people who can best describe what feelings or emotions are. For a musician, all feelings can be described by using seven notes. For a painter, all emotions can be represented by using three colors. All lives can be described with four colors or four notes [see Book of Life (III)]. The human being's genes and the bacterium's genes are constructed with identical building blocks, but their nucleotide sequence is different. In other words, all lives are singing their life song with four universal notes, or they are painting their self-portrait with four universal colors. Furthermore, without feelings, lives are unable to interact with their environment. The emotions and intelligence are closely related. We are unable to detect the emotions of a bacterium or a virus. Nevertheless, we have no rights to deny that they have emotions simply because of our own ignorance.

7) All lives possess soul. Buddhists say that "all" lives have souls, but Christian doctrines say that only humans have soul. Today, there is no way to detect the existence of the soul by any instruments developed by modern sciences. We can measure time, space, material flow, and we can observe the reproduction processes. But, what is the soul? All living lives are trapped in space and time. Is soul also trapped in space-time? If it is, then the soul should possess mass (all things — lives or lifeless material — possess mass if they are trapped in space-time), and it could be detected by physical instruments. So far, soul is unobservable. Therefore, the soul cannot be a thing or a being. A thing has to occupy space. A being has to be trapped in time train. Is the existence of souls permitted by physics law? The answer is "no" according to the traditional physics. But, the answer is "yes" according to "Super Unified Theory — a theory of everything, for lifeless particles, lives, God, the creation before the creation." The region of "after death" is unobservable. But, the unobservable principle is one of the corner stones of Super Unified Theory. Again, we have no right to deny the existence of soul simply because we are unable to observe it. Actually, the existence of soul for all lives is a theoretical consequence in the Super Unified Theory.

III

In summary, the difference between life and lifeless is great. Darwin wrote, "The most humble organism is something much higher than the inorganic dust under our feet; and no one with an unbiased mind can study any living creature, however humble, without being struck with enthusiasm at its marvellous structure and properties." Life is indeed more than an assembled machinery or an orderly controlled chemical tank. Life has the power of self-nutrition, but lifelessness does not. Life has the power of self-reproduction, but lifelessness does not. The difference between life and lifelessness is so great, greater than the difference between heaven and hell.

But, there are many links between life and lifelessness. All lives can use lifeless material as food and nutrition. All lives must die, returning to lifelessness. The link between life and death is the most profound evidence for the connection between the alive and the lifeless.

The lifeless also dies. All rocks will crumble into dust eventually; they die slowly. On the contrary, death separates the alive form lifeless not only as far apart as earth and heaven, but it is also an irreversible process. A candle fire can be quenched and be lit again, but a plucked rose must wither. Is life an eruptible bubble imbedded in a huge lifeless background or is this "lifeless" background actually alive?

According to many religions, the soul is living inside the body of every life when the life is alive, and the soul goes to heaven after the death of the material body.

In Super Unified Theory, heaven is an infinity; all souls converge into it. Heaven is a different manifestation of God Himself. God and Heaven is one entity. But, our ever-living God does not show any attribute possessed by a corporeal life. God is eternally alive. Indeed, death is not a grand canyon that separates the alive and the lifeless but a link between them, uniting our soul with God. Therefore, the difference between the natural and the supernatural, between the material and the spiritual, and between the lifeless and the alive is only in degree or in kind but not in origin. In Book of Life (III), I will discuss what soul is.

Gong's book has unified not only four physical forces, which was the lost dream of Einstein, but also all opposites: science and religions, reasoning and faith. His book is the one and the only TOE, the "Theory of Everything." The TOE always points to the direction where future leads. The TOE always takes us to the future where the eternal truth resides.

—Hu Chen-Ming, Professor of Mathematics.

Book of Truth (II)

Conservation laws,
The creation before the first creation,
and the Ghost Partner

All lives face death. Even stars with a size of our solar system will die and collapse into a neutron ball, which can be as small as a single family house. The whole galaxy can also collapse into a black hole. Black holes were named black hole because no lights can escape from them. However, regardless of its massive mass, the black hole also will disintegrate eventually. Can anything last forever? Can anything be conserved?

II

The concept of conservation is very simple. If you have five dollars in your pocket today and a same amount of money remains in your pocket one day or one year from now, then we say that the money in your pocket is conserved for one day or one year. This five dollar in your pocket does not need to be the same five dollar bill; the money conservation remains if the five dollar bill turns into five dollars worth of coins.

Scientists have developed a precise procedure to test the conservation laws. If the measurement of the mass of a gold bar in America is the same as its measurement in China, then its mass is conserved after a transporting operation. If the measurement of the mass of the same gold bar taken 1000 years ago is the same as the measurement of today, then its mass is conserved through time. Many conservation laws are the cornerstones of modern sciences, such as momentum conservation law, angular momentum conservation law, mass conservation law, energy conservation law, and mass-energy conservation law.

These conservation laws guarantee that the mass of a life will not disappear into nowhere after its death. All its mass or the material part of a life will be returned to earth without any loss or gain. The only observable loss for a death is the stoppage of the material flow and the disintegration of its mass body. Does soul conserve? Does the soul remain as an individual identity after the death of a life? Or, does the soul disintegrate into pieces the same as the mass body?

So far, all conservation laws listed above are proved to be correct in the laboratories. They also should have been true in laboratories millions of years ago, and they will remain true in laboratories for millions of years to come. But, millions of years is a very short period compared to the life of our universe. Do these conservation laws remain true through out the life time of our universe? The answer is "No." The breaking down of the conservation law can be understood easily. If you spend your five dollars tomorrow but earn another five dollars back day after tomorrow, then the money seems to be conserved at two points, today and the day after tomorrow. But, the money conservation does break down after the time you spent your money but before you earn the same amount back. Therefore, if the time instrument can only measure time between a small interval, then many events can become unobservable. All conservation laws can break down between the two observable end points although they remain to be true at these two points. All conservation laws were not true at the point of creation (the big bang), and they will not remain true at the point of "The End" (the big crunch). Actually, those conservation laws are not true even now regardless of how many proofs we find in our laboratories. They are true in our laboratories that can be as big as a galaxy, which is still too primitive and too small compared with the whole universe. For our universe as a whole, much of mass is created continuously from nowhere; I will explain what "nowhere" is in the following discussions. One day, our universe will collapse into a big fire ball because of the continuous increasing mass and gravity. This prediction does not come from faith but from a new truth machine.

In order to understand this new truth machine, we need first to understand some of the following issues, which have been discussed by traditional physicists.

1) The universe started from a big fire ball; they call it the Big Bang. This is true. But, where did this fire ball come from? Traditional scientists did not know the answer. For them, therefore,

such a question has no meaning and does not deserve an answer. If anyone tries to give an explanation, they will surely view it as fiction and non-science.

2) Our universe is expanding outward. This is also true. But, what is the outside of the existing universe? There is "nothing" able to exist outside the universe by definition. The definition of the universe is a "whole" body of things and phenomena, and there is no external vantage outside the universe. Space-time represents mass. If the outside of the universe has "mass," then it is part of the universe. If the outside of the universe has "space," then it is part of the universe. If the outside of universe has "time," then it is also part of the universe. The only thing can exist outside the universe is "nothing." An outward expanding universe has to convert "nothing" into something, mass, space, and time.

At the point of the big bang, the gravity force and thermal expansion were at equilibrium for a while, but "some how" (see explanation below) the thermal expansion force overpowered the gravity force, and it pushed part of the fire ball into "nothing"—the outside of the fire ball. But, what is "nothing?" Time and space are closely related. When space expanded, the time also moved forward. When time moved forward, then both space and mass were created. The space-time interaction creates new mass. When the total mass of the universe increases to a critical point, then the gravity force will overpower the expanding momentum, and the universe will collapse. The newly created mass is filling in the newly expanded space, and they are exactly balanced without disturbing any other area. Therefore, the conservation laws seem to be preserved in any observable area. For example, you had five dollars in savings 30 years ago and your savings remain as five dollars today, then your savings account is conserved. Your son was born 20 years ago, and he had zero cents then but has five dollars of savings today. Between you and your son, the total savings has doubled, but your savings account remains to be conserved. If your son's savings account is unobservable for you because he does not wish to share his private business with you, then you will easily conclude that the saving account in general is conserved.

3) From all known data and measurements, our universe does not have enough mass to collapse itself. This is true too. Our universe is still growing and not has yet reached the critical point. Only a handful of physicists believes the universe will expand forever. Others believe that our universe will eventually collapse into a fire

ball again. But so far, this universe simply does not have enough observable mass to contract this expanding universe. Therefore, many physicists try to invent some hidden angels that are called dark matter, such as neutrino, super symmetry particles. So far, all their attempts have failed.

The evolution theory describes a process of how lives evolve after the creation. Actually, the physics laws are also evolving through time. Many far away galaxies are billions of light years away. The images we are seeing today are billions of years old. At that time (early stage of our universe), the gravity force-constant was a lot larger than what we observe today. Therefore, those old galaxies seem to lack the necessary mass to hold themselves together by using today's gravity force standard. Those old galaxies did not fall apart because the gravity factor (constant) was much larger then. The gravitational constant G is not really a constant throughout the life of our universe.

III

It is very stupid of anyone for not believing the big fire ball story, which is the favored son of our modern physics. But, it is equally stupid of any physicist who buries his head in the sand to ignore the question of where the fire ball came from.

God created God all by himself. The real procedure is that "God created Holy Ghost, then Holy Ghost created God." These statements seem to make no sense at all. But, a similar procedure takes place in our daily life all the time.

For example, I do not have a house, and I do not have any money. Actually, I have "NOTHING." And, thank God; I do have "NOTHING." The word "NOTHING" is the first key. Now, I am going to create (build) a house (something) from "nothing." The only way to do it is by promising that I will pay the banker back all the principal plus interest if he lends me some money. With borrowed money, I turn "nothing" into "something" (a new house), but a ghost partner is also created at the same time. The name of this ghost partner is called mortgage payment book. Unfortunately, the ghost partner always grows bigger than its real partner. If the cost of your newly built house is $100,000, the ghost partner will likely grow to $300,000. This growth factor of the ghost partner is the second key of how our universe has grown to today's size. The third key for creation is called fluctuation; this characteristic is inherited by us, and we find it everywhere. We call it chaos. The general perception for chaos is not very good. But, chaos is not really bad. For example, the badly needed spring storm is caused by chaos. The difference between chaos and order is only one hairline thick. The television picture becomes chaos if the adjustment knob is off slightly from its normal position. But this chaotic picture that is completely unrecognizable contains identical information and signals the same as the beautiful picture before it that has been scrambled. Many cable television stations do scramble their signals to prevent the piracy; the chaotic picture was descrambled for every paid customer. Actually, the chaotic state is often the building blocks of all orderly states. A sand castle can be beautiful and has a beautiful order, but it is built with orderless sand that has a chaotic state. Chaos is not only an important part of our life, but it is the origin of all lives. We do have more chaos than order in this world and in our life. Furthermore, the brain wave of a healthy person is very chaotic. On the contrary, the brain wave of a person who is in a coma is very orderly. In other words, if you have an orderly brain wave, then your days are numbered. On the other hand, if your brain wave is very chaotic, then you have more time to live. Chaos and order are the two sides of the same coin. Actually, chaos is the base of the pyramid, and orderliness is the vertex on the top of the pyramid. The subject of chaos is so important and significant for the creation process that it deserves a whole chapter all by itself. See Book of Truth (V) — Chaos.

So, God has one soul and three manifestations.

The soul is called "NOTHING." Therefore, God was there, and He did not need to be created.

The first manifestation is called material (the entire universe), and it contains three items — mass, time, and space.

The second is called "Ghost Partner," and it is the gravitation.

The third is called "Chaos," and all orders were born by and from chaos.

At the point before the first creation, there is "nothing" — an absolute "Vacuum;" it represents an absolute zero energy. At this stage, there is no "Time" or "Space" because time and space are

"something," which is not "nothing." Then, the "chaos" separates
the "vacuum" into two small energy bubbles. One carries a very
small amount of positive energy; the other carries an equal amount
of negative energy. For this system as a whole, there is still "nothing"
(absolute vacuum); the positive cancelled with the negative; therefore,
nothing has changed. No reason we know is able to prevent this
type of chaos from taking place. Chaos itself is "nothing" [see Book
of Truth (V) — Chaos], and only "nothing" can exist without being
created. In physics, the positive energy can often manifest into a
particle, such as proton. As soon as this first particle was created,
four items were also created at the same time, and there is no way
to separate them.

The first item is space. A particle always occupies a space.

The second item is time regardless of how short lived this particle is.

The third item is the ghost partner.

The fourth item is a growth phenomenon. At the point of creation, the energy carried by particle (such as proton) is exactly the
same as the negative energy carried by the ghost partner. The particle's mass in energy. The "space" it occupied and the "time" it lasted
are also energy. All those energies have to be borrowed from the
ghost partner. There was nothing before, and it has to remain to
be nothing all the time. Therefore, for every minute that goes by,
the ghost partner will grow because time is also energy.

When this first particle has died, only mass energy can be released
back into the system, and it is many folds smaller than the ghost
partner, which has been growing constantly during the particle's
lifetime. For the system as a whole, there is energy left over which
is the interest payment paid during the life time of the first particle
for its enjoyment of possessing "space" and "time" (Life is not free).
This left over energy should manifest into two or more anti-particles.
When this small universe (more than one particle) has died, its ghost
partner will grow even bigger and manifest into a bigger universe
filled with particles (anti-anti-particles). And, so it goes continuously. Matter and anti-matter alternately appear in each big bang, and
the size of the universe will increase by a factor of 2 or more during
each cycle.

Today, no anti-matter galaxy exists in this entire universe. In
physics, there is no explanation found of why our universe prefers
matter to its identical twin brother (anti-matter). And, why did

God create two identical twin brothers (matter and anti-matter)? But, our entire universe is made of only one of them. Now, we all know the answer. After our universe faces the judgement day and collapses into a big fire ball, the next universe will be constructed with our twin brother (anti-matter).

IV

I have shown you the procedure of creating "something" from "nothing." The traditional conservation laws are not true at the point of this kind of creation. Nonetheless, "nothing" has to remain to be "nothing." The "nothing" conservation law has to be preserved, and it does. I am going to use a simple example to demonstrate this point.

I am going to use "green" dollars to represent "matter," and use "red" dollars to represent the "ghost partner," which can manifest into anti-matter after the matter universe has collapsed. At the beginning, there is "nothing." When one green dollar materialized, caused by chaos, from "nothing," a red dollar has to be created at the same time to maintain the whole system of remaining to be "nothing." For every "minute" of existence of green dollar, more red dollars are created because the time is money (energy) too. I am going to arbitrarily choose "3" as the life time factor. When one green dollar ends its life journey, the one red dollar has grown into 3 red dollars. At the point of green-red unification, 2 red dollars are left over and it can manifest into 2 anti-particles, and its ghost partner (green dollars) also will start with 2 and begin to grow from there. Without recognizing the existence of the ghost partner, the "nothing" seems not conserved. But, at the point of eternity (infinity), the "nothing" conservation law is clearly preserved. This point can be demonstrated with a green and a red series.

Green	1	4	16	258	_____	_____

Red	2	8	32	128	_____	_____

With finite number of cycles, the green and red are not in balance. For example, with 3 cycles each, the sum for green is $1+4+16=21$, and the sum for red is $2+8+32=42$. But, at the infinite point, the sum of $1+4+16+ . . + . . .$ is the same as $2+8+32+ . . + . . .$ Red and green are indeed equal at the point of infinity.

There are two very important points. The imbalance between
red and green in any finite number of cylces is the driving force
for the continuous creation and for the existence of the material
universe. Without this imbalance, our universe can return to "nothing"
and stay in "nothingness" for a long time. For infinite cycles, the
red and the green are in balance; therefore, the "nothing" conservation law is still preserved.

There are also some special meanings for colors and eternity.
I will discuss colors in the Book of Truth (III) — Forces, Building
Blocks, and Colors. I will discuss the meaning of eternity in the
Book of Life (III) — Soul, Eternity, and Colors.

V

For two thousand years, philosophy and religion competed for
supremacy. Science was only a small branch in philosophy four hundred years ago. But, today, many scientists have labeled philosophy
as "speculation" and religion as "superstition."

Freud wrote, "It asserts that there is no other source of knowledge
of the universe, but the intellectual manipulation of carefully verified
observations, in fact, what is called research, and that no knowledge
can be obtained from revelation, intuition, or inspiration."

The fact is that science itself is in chaos. The foundations of
all sciences are a few axioms and principles, which are accepted
mainly on faith. All mathematics is constructed with many definitions, which are results of "free will." Two completely contradictory
definitions can, in fact, produce two equally valid mathematics.

The methodology of hypothesis, prediction and verification, is
indeed useful and valid in time- and space-bonded domain, and
it would be foolish to think otherwise. But, our universe is much
bigger and much more than just time and space. The existence of
God is very much self-evident. Science rejects a theory of God, not
because it is able to disprove the existence of God, but it thinks
God has no place in science. How wrong this notion can be!
Mathematics is not and cannot be developed from our own free
will; it comes from God's free will. The validity of reasoning, induction or deduction, is not proved or invented by us but is guaranteed
by God.

Only a new truth machine is able to help us attain the utmost truth. Now is the time to construct a new truth machine, and it contains three parts.

The first is the self-evidence principle. Many axioms and principles, indemonstrable truths, are self-evident, and they are accepted by scientists mainly with faith. Furthermore, the connection between assumptions and conclusions in syllogism is also indemonstrable and must be perceived intuitively.

Aristotle wrote, "It is by intuition that we obtain the primary premises."

But, the most self-evident fact is the existence of God.

Tolstoy wrote, "If He were not, . . . , you and I would not be speaking of Him, . . . Why didst thou, and why did the whole world, conceive the idea of the existence of such an incomprehensible Being, a Being all-powerful, eternal, and infinite in all His attributes? . . . To know Him is hard . . . For ages, for our forefather Adam to our own day, we labor to attain that knowledge and are still infinitely far from our aim; but in our lack of understanding we see only our weakness and His greatness . . ."

That the water flows from high to low places is self-evident. Newton's laws are also very much self-evident, especially for physicists. All natural phenomena are self-evident; they are more clear and obvious for some trained eyes than others, but the difference is in degree, not in kind. This ability to identify those self-evident truths is a Godsend gift.

Spinoza wrote, "The human mind possesses an adequate knowledge of eternal and infinite essence of God."

Locke wrote, "We have as much reason to be satisfied with our notion of immaterial spirit, as with our notion of body, and the existence of the one as well as the other. . . . But whichever of these complex idea be clearest, that of body, or immaterial spirit, this is evident, that the simple ideas that make them up are no other than what we have received from sensation or reflection; and so is it of all our other ideas of substances, even of God Himself."

Indeed, each of us receives our ability of understanding, whether through sensation or reasoning, from God. There are no additional steps needed to improve this Godsend gift. We, however, should connect every individual intelligence into a collective knowledge through a process, which I call it—conviction in common, a consensus. Often, our convictions that evolve and grow when our visions are improved by accumulated knowledge are able to probe the deeper self-evidence. The origin of reasoning is a Godsend gift; the growth of knowledge can be built by using the method of conviction in common.

The second is the hypotheses principle, the interplay between theory and experiment. But, who gives the scientists the ability to reason or to judge a theory and an external evidence? The validity of reasoning cannot be guaranteed by a step-by-step construction unless its foundation is also valid. The foundation of this hypothesis principle is in fact fundamentally wrong in its traditional sense although it does produce many limited truths in the space- and time-bonded domain. It is wrong in principle but right in reality. This principle becomes valid only because God Who is denied and rejected by science guarantees the validity of its foundation. The origin of our "free will" to choose a hypothesis or a definition also resides in God.

The third is the indivisibility (unification) principle. All things come out from God and will return to God. The self-evidence principle and the hypotheses principle have to unite to be able to reach the utmost truth. The principle of consistency alone can no longer guarantee the validity of a theory. An obvious contradiction also can no longer guarantee the invalidity of a theory. Order and chaos are united as a whole. We can no longer reject or deny a notion simply because we cannot find a place for it in reality. Our reality is only a very small part of the true world. We can no longer use either self-evidence principle or hypothesis principle alone to probe the utmost truth. We often have to unite two contradictory phenomena into a unified existence. We are unable to perform a laboratory experiment for any existence, which is immaterial and immutable. But, we are able to understand its existence by a procedure, which I call it — example in kinds. We are able to understand the existence of the ghost partner with an example of buying a house, and accept it with "faith." The principle of example in kinds is much more than the methodology of induction, which attains a general truth with an inductive leap, from only some observed particulars that are the same kind. The principle of example in kinds leaps over the boundaries of different kinds, science, philosophy, and religion. It is also much more than the methodology of analogy, which depends on exact similarity and resemblance. When the similarity is less perfect, the analogy is less conclusive.

The validity of the principle of example in kinds is because of our "faith:" that of believing there is one and only one God, therefore, one and only one utmost truth. All facts are only different views of the same truth. The principle of example in kinds is the direct consequence of the principle of indivisibility [See Book of Truth (IV)].

Obviously, there is a danger that someone will use this princi- ple, "example in kind," in an abusive manner to promote some ab- surd opinions. Fortunately, the interplay of all three principles keeps this kind of nonsense out of the domain of true knowledge.

In summary, our instinct, a Godsend gift, is the origin of reason- ing. The conviction in common is a method for constructing knowledge. Our free will, another Godsend gift, is the lease on life for hypothesis principle, the interplay between theory and experi- ment. Our faith, demanded by God, is the only way to understand the unified existence between chaos and orderliness, between evil and goodness, between wicked and righteousness, and between the one and the many. All three are, in fact, one. With all three, we are able to understand the utmost truth, our Almighty God. I under- stand; therefore, I worship.

Many people have difficulty imagining the existence and the meaning of the higher dimensions beyond the familiar three space dimensions. In fact, all dimensions are just labels, which identify and describe events and existence.

Book of Life (II)
Dimensions, Colors, and Unilogy

The word "dimension" is scientific jargon, but it can be understood easily with common language. A long thread has one dimension because it represents a length. A sheet of paper has two dimensions because it represents an area. A box has three dimensions because it represents a volume.

A one-dimensional subject can always be described with one coordinate (variable), and traditionally we use x-axis as the first dimension. A two-dimensional subject can always be described with two coordinates, such as x-axis and y-axis. A three-dimensional subject can always be described with three coordinates, such as x-axis, y-axis, and z-axis. If a subject is moving in a three-dimensional space, then a fourth-dimension (time) is needed to describe its movement and to locate its position at any given time. We seem to be able to describe all particles' activities with 4 and only 4 dimensions. Actually, 11 dimensions are needed to describe the entire universe, such as forces between particles, lives, cultures, death of a life, and everything else.

II

Many people have difficulty imagining the existence and the meaning of the higher dimensions beyond the familiar three space dimensions. In fact, all dimensions are just labels, which identify and describe events and existence. Let us imagine that an astronaut who comes from our neighboring galaxy has an assignment to report our activities back to his planet. I call him Mr. Smith. He begins his case study by observing Mr. Johnson's (earth man) daily activities. It is very easy to record Mr. Johnson's movements by using 3 space coordinates and one time coordinate. But, very soon, Mr. Smith finds out that Mr. Johnson's activities are more complicated than

4 dimensions can handle. He often sees that Mr. Johnson goes to market places, banks, and factory. He does not know what these activities are about. After a detailed study, he decides to use a "green" label to describe this activity, and he assigns a "green 50" as the present state of Mr. Johnson. Next day, Mr. Johnson receives a pay check, and the green label is changed to "green 60." The next week, Mr. Johnson bought a new car, and the green label is changed to "green 40."

Then, he finds out something else about Mr. Johnson. Mr. Johnson often laughs, smiles, and sometimes gets angry. Mr. Smith does not know what emotion is, but it is obviously a new phenomenon. So, he uses a "red" label to describe this phenomenon, and "red 50" is assigned to represent the present state of Mr. Johnson.

Mr. Johnson often ignores many strangers but hugs many friends. Mr. Smith does not know what social relation is, and all 4 dimensions and two new color labels are unable to explain these activities. So, he uses a "yellow" label to describe these activities. "Yellow 0" is for stranger. "Yellow 100" is for husband and wife.

After reviewing the last 50 years' records, Mr. Smith finds out that Mr. Johnson was once a baby. He also detects that Mr. Johnson's body has changed. The body change can be measured by using 3 space coordinates and one time coordinate, during the first 20 years. After that, many changes—such as illness, mental maturity, and hair color changes—in Mr. Johnson's body and mind cannot be described by any known labels, and this must be a new phenomenon. It should be represented by a new color. But, Mr. Smith only brought three color labels with him. He writes a "G1" on a sheet of white paper to represent the fourth color, which he calls aging or death color. "G1-100" represents excellent health. "G1-0" represents death.

For every few years, Ms. Johnson gave birth to a baby. This is definitely a new phenomenon. Mr. Smith does not know what kind of force is behind this phenomenon. He uses "G2" as the fifth color label for these events.

Mr. Smith also realizes that Mr. Johnson is the descendant of his ancestors who no longer exist in a material form. Their existence is undeniable not only for the past but also for the present time.

He uses "G3" as the sixth color label to identify the existence of Mr. Johnson's ancestors who are still in the memory of many people.

With 3 space-coordinates, one time-coordinate, and 6 color labels, Mr. Smith sends the following report back to his planet.
"Mr. Johnson (G3): Time—February 20th, 1989: $X = 0$, $Y = 0$, $Z = 0$: Yellow 100 (G2-1): Red 100, Green 60, G1-50."

This message can be translated to earthly language as follow: "On February 20th, 1989 (time), Ms. Johnson (Yellow 100) had a baby (G2-1) at home ($X = 0$, $Y = 0$, $Z = 0$). He (G3—descendant of Johnson) is very happy (Red 100). His financial situation (Green 60) is good. His health (G1-50) is good."
With 4 dimensions and 6 colors, Mr. Smith is able to document the detailed activities for all lives from past to present, and he can even probe the future. X, Y, Z, and time are for locating the body of a life. The green label is for identifying the material flow (food, water, money, etc.). The red label is for identifying the emotion of a life. The yellow label is for identifying the social relation of a life. The G1 color is for identifying the states of being, such as health, illness, or death. The G2 color is for identifying the creation of new lives—reproduction. The G3 color is for identifying the soul of a deceased life. G1, G2 and G3 are colors, which identify the generations of lives.

Those color labels are also dimensions. We have always called x, y, z, and time as dimensions, and we will continue to do so, but it is easier to call those color dimensions as colors. Furthermore, colors have a lot more meanings than dimensions have; they are special dimensions.

III

So far, Mr. Smith, an imaginary astronaut, has arbitrarily assigned six colors for lives. There is a big difference between "discover" and "assign." The above example is only intended to explain what color labels are and how we can use them to discover and describe what kind of meanings lives does possess. We shall discover the true meaning of color dimensions by asking the answers from all lives.

The color dimensions can be precisely described by Topology, which is a branch of mathematics. Topology is also called plastics mathematics. For example, a balloon ball can be changed into a cylinder through a continuous deformation process. Therefore, every cylinder is a topological sphere. For a balloon with a head, arms, and legs, it is still the same as a topological ball because those parts are stretched out from the ball. With a continuous deformation process, it can return to a spherical ball.

But, there is no way of changing a ball into a donut, which is called a torus in Topology, through a continuous deformation process. In Topology, a ball and a donut are two distinctive objects, and there is no way to transform one to the other. Again, since mathematicians do not know how to transform a ball into a donut topologically, therefore, such a transformation has no meaning to them. Indeed, most of the scientists can only study a subject, which is tangible or imaginable. They always bury their heads in the sand for any issue, which seems not to obey the rules they invented.

Actually, everyone is capable of performing this transformation by using a scissors and a piece of thread.

First, cut a plastic donut open along the largest diameter to form a cylindrical surface.

Then, sew up both ends of the cylinder.

Finally, pull the thread tight and squeeze the seam into a point. I call this a black point.

Now, we have transformed a donut into a ball. The only difference between this donut ball and the topological ball is that this donut ball has two tightened knots (black points). So, the "topological donut" is equivalent to a "topological ball" plus two "black points."

There is a special characteristic, which is called an Euler number for all topological objects. If two different shaped objects are topologically equivalent, then they will have the same Euler number. Only topologically different objects have a different Euler number. The Euler number for a ball is 0 (zero), and it is 2 (two) for a donut.

Amazingly, the number of black points (knots) after every "scissors and thread operation" has the same value as the Euler number. I call this "scissors and thread operation" a "Unilogical transformation."

Euler number is the only identification number needed for distinguishing the different shapes of topological objects. But, all those objects can be transformed from one to another through a unilogical transformation. So, all objects, (a ball, a donut, a cylinder, etc.) should be unilogically equal, and there should be a unilogical number for all of those objects. Indeed, we do have such a number. I define "unilogical number" for any object as Euler number minus the number of black points of an object after it has unilogically transformed into a topological ball, and the valve of the unilogical number is 0 (zero) for all objects.

IV

In Book of Truth (II), I have pointed out that all materials were manifested out of "nothing." Now, I have also proved that all shapes of objects were manifested out of a unilogical number, which has a value of 0 (zero). How wonderful, the mathematical value for "nothing" is proved to be zero.

All of these discussions lead us to understand a very important phenomenon. Life is the result of a unilogical transformation, from a ball into a donut. A fertilized egg will multiply into a ball shaped mass, and we call it embryo. Suddenly, this ball shaped embryo will stop the outward expansion, but many cells flow from the outer surface of the ball into the center of the ball. An internal tube is formed, and it becomes the internal organs of a life. After this transformation, we call the embryo a fetus. This embryo-fetus transformation is actually a ball-donut transformation. Most of the lives have a topological shape as a donut, with an internal tube, which has two or more opening which connects it to its outer surface, but all of them were started from a single ball shaped cell. Many lives perform this unilogical transformation all the time.

This phenomenon has a direct impact on the meaning of color dimensions. There is a very famous theorem, which is called Four color theorem. For all the countries on earth (which is a ball), four and only four colors are needed to color all countries that do not share the same color with any neighboring countries. The real meaning of this theorem is that we are able to create unlimited number of balls with only four colors, and each of them has its own set of color pattern, which is distinctively different from those of all other balls. The individuality can, therefore, be possible for each life.

For a donut, seven colors are needed to do the same job. If a life form has a topological shape as a donut, then seven color dimensions are needed to describe it. Seven colors are needed to create the individuality. So far, Mr. Smith, an imaginary astronaut, has arbitrarily assigned six colors for lives. In the Book of Life (III), I will discuss the true meaning of the color dimensions by asking the answers from all lives.

Book of Truth (III)

Forces, Building blocks, and Colors

We all know what forces are. When your fist flies through the air and lands on your enemy's nose, we call this action — "force." An ideal that flows through society also will create a big force. It is so obvious that there are physical forces, mental forces, and culture forces. So far traditional physics is unable to analyze the mental forces, the lively forces, and the cultural forces. From this stand point, traditional physics is far from understanding the utmost truth, but their achievements of understanding the physical forces do provide some important clues for understanding all forces.

II

All forces are the results of flows, which can be composed of material, particles, ideals, love, or hatred. Today, four physical forces are partially understood by physicists. Actually, those four forces can be easily understood with common language. We all know about the electrical force, which is the result of electron-flow. The harmful radiation decay is caused by a force, which is called "weak force" because it is much weaker than the force that bonds the particles into a nucleus. The force that bonds the particles into a nucleus is called "strong force." The force that prevents us from flying into the sky is called gravitational force.

It is not very easy to detect the flows that produce the weak, the strong, and the gravitational forces. The weak and strong forces were finally partially understood through a "football theory." According to electrical force, protons should repulse each other because they all possess positive electrical charges. Therefore, all nucleuses that are mainly composed of protons should fly apart, but most of them are stable. A stronger force among protons must exist to overcome the repulsive electrical force.

In general, man and woman attract each other. Sometimes, many men are concentrated into a small space (such as in a football field) with the same situation as protons in a nucleus. These football players are attracted into a small area by a subject, which is called "football." Instead of repulsing each other by the normal sexual rules, the "football" bonds those men together. It is highly likely that all protons are also bonded by their "football" that was named "Boson." So, both weak and strong forces are the results of boson-flow.

Physicists are now trying to find the "football" that generates the gravitational force. They call this imaginary gravitational football—"Graviton," but all their attempts failed to detect such an object. Actually, the gravitational force is generated by a flowing object, which is called "time." When a mass rests stationary, it is actually moving from the stand point of "time," and the force that moves this mass in the time coordinate is gravitation. For example, a pen rests stationary in my hand at 1 p.m. and remains there one hour later. The pen did not move during the one hour according to the space coordinates, but it did move according to the time coordinate. In the space-time frame, this pen was at the point that had a coordinate as (my hand, 1 p.m.); one hour later, its coordinate has changed to (my hand, 2 p.m.). So, this stationary pen has moved from one coordiante to a new coordinate in the space-time domain. This movement is caused by time—flow, which is the football for gravitational force. But, this easy concept and fact is not recognized by physicists today. These stiff-necked physicists waste much tax payers' money and their own energy and time to study the imaginary graviton, which does not exist.

Einstein's special relativity theory has been proved to be valid in the laboratory many times. Our civilization advanced with a quantum leap into the electronic and nuclear age with some helps from this special relativity theory. But, this elegant theory also became a major road block for half a century. Now, all scientists still believe that a mass body can never move with light speed because they "think" that special relativity theory prohibits it from happening. Actually, special relativity theory does not prohibit a mass body from moving with light speed, but it prohibits a mass body from moving with light speed "relative to" other mass bodies or coordinates. The wrong interpretation by Einstein and many scientists has prevented scientists from understanding the gravitational force. A "rest" mass body is moving with light speed from the stand point of "time" while it is indeed in a state of stillness in space. Again, this is a classic example that some absolutely wrong assumptions and interpretations are able to produce some correct predictions. The truth is that the predictions and their assumptions do not really have any logical "connection." There are many similar examples in religions. All religions try to make a "connection" with the same God through different sets of assumptions. Each of them develops its own colorful culture, but many of their assumptions do not really have any logical connection with God.

Now, the creation process is very clear. The essence of God is nothingness and chaos. Material and its ghost partner came out of nothing because of chaos. The mass conservation law is valid for all of the material world, but the energy of its ghost partner continues to grow as long as the material world stays alive. The material world has to pay a price to its ghost partner for its lease on life. When the lease ends, the material world will be unable to balance its debt, therefore, the ghost partner will materialize into an anti-matter world. This indebted and imbalance cycle goes on. The universe will finally grow into today's size. The gravitational force is the mortgage book for the transaction between this universe and its ghost partner. The commodity in this transaction is time. Therefore, time is the force-carrier for gravitational force.

III

Forces are glues, and this universe is constructed by gluing some basic building blocks together. Traditional sciences find three layers of building blocks. In the Super Unified Theory, there are four layers of building block structures.

All materials are constructed by approximate 100 different kind of atoms. Atoms are the outer layer. All atoms are constructed by neutrons, protons, electrons, and bosons. Neutrons, protons, and electrons are the second layer. The third layer is a bit more complicated. Electron is unchanged, but neutrons or protons are constructed by some third layer subjects, which are called "quarks." At this point, something new is discovered, and they are called "colors." Neutron, proton, boson and electron are colorless, but quarks have three colors, red, yellow, and blue. Today, the quark color is a worldwide accepted physics concept. Furthermore, our entire universe is constructed with two and only two kinds of light quark, but six different kinds of quark are found in the laboratory. What are those four extra quarks for?

Again, not only life forms are evolving through time, but the basic building blocks of the universe also change with time. Those four heavy quarks were the building blocks at a very early stage of the universe. Today, only two kinds of light quark are needed. At the beginning of the creation and before the explosion of the big bang, the entire universe was at an infinite state. At this infinite state, proton, neutron or even quarks cannot exist; the entire universe is made of subparticles that are called prequarks, the building blocks of quarks. In Super Unified Theory, there is a fourth layer, prequarks. There are two kinds of prequark: one is Vacutron that is vacuum or nothingness, the other is Angultron that is the distortion of space. Angultron is the manifestation of space and time.

At the beginning, there is "Nothing," no space, no time. When something was created from "Nothing," space, time and mass also appeared. The ghost partner (gravitation) also appeared. After many cycles of big bang and big crunch, the universe grows [See Book of Truth (II)]. Right after the big bang, a very important transformation took place; the universe was transformed from an infinite state to a finite state. During this infinite-finite transformation, quarks were formed. Actually, there were three sub-transformations to complete this infinite to finite transformation. These three sub-transformations are three generations. Each generation is composed of two quarks. Therefore, six quarks represent three generations of the evolution stages. I call these three generations — genecolors, G1, G2, G3.

Amazingly, there are also seven colors — colorless, red, yellow, blue, G1, G2, G3 — in physics. These color dimensions provide us a clue and an opportunity to unify physics laws and the laws that created lives. See Book of Truth (IV) and Book of Life (III).

How wonderful, we have traced the building blocks of our universe all the way back to God who is "nothing" and "chaos." Vacutron is nothingness, and Angultron is created by chaos. Please do not feel offended by these words of "nothing" and "chaos." They seem to have some bad or negative meaning in our earthly language, but they are as holy as anything ever can be. Please do not be disturbed by the earthly meaning of these words, and try to understand them from the logic this book provides.

Often, words can provide bad information and misunderstanding. Most people are afraid of some unfamiliar words, such as quarks, neutrinos. Quark is just a word invented by some physicists, and it just represents a kind of building block for protons. Vacutron and Angultron are the building blocks for quarks. If you are interested in the details of the "Chromodynamics" that describes color forces, please refer to my book "Super Unified Theory" — it has an ISBN 0-916713-01-6 and a Library of Congress catalog card number 84-90325.

IV

Nonetheless, the structure of our universe is not any more complicated than the newspaper that you read daily. If you can imagine that the newspaper in your hand is a small universe, then you also can imagine that every story in the paper is a galaxy. And, every paragraph can be viewed as a star. Every sentence can be viewed as an atom. Every word can be viewed as protons, neutron, etc. Then, 26 letters and 12 punctuation marks can be viewed as quarks. Can you imagine that there is one more layer under the quarks? If you put some printed letters under the microscope, you will find that every letter is constructed by many small white dots and color dots. The white dots can be viewed as "Vacutron" or "nothing." The color dots can be viewed as "Angultron."

So far, all physicists are unable to describe the cultural forces with their force equation. A unified force equation has to be able to describe all phenomena, and it does. The following is the description of the unified force equation.

The denominator part of the unified force equation is a "product" of "the effected space or area" and "the duration of time." The farther away from the force source, the weaker the force will be at that point. The longer time elapsed, the weaker the force remains at that time. For example, a live rock concert (without TV broadcasting) has a big impact in the auditorium when it is going on, and its impact is dramatically reduced outside the auditorium and after the concert is over.

The numerator part of the unified force equation is a "coupling factor," which represents how strong the force "source" is. For example, a Chinese novel has a very strong coupling power among Chinese, but it has very little influence among English speaking people. Most of the time, this coupling factor is a constant, and its force will decrease quickly when time elapses and the distance increases. Sometimes, a force source is a life, and its influence lasts throughout both space and time. For example, the salvation from Jesus Christ has lasted for two thousand years worldwide. So, the coupling factor for the teaching of Jesus is increasing proportionally to the elapsed time and expanded space. The longer the time elapsed, the stronger the coupling factor is. Therefore, the force and power that comes from Jesus Christ is a never ending force.

The unified force equation is as follow: unified force equals coupling factor times Plank's constant divided by (the effected space times the duration of the time). With this equation, not only the cultural forces can be clearly described, but gravitational force and electric force are also easily unified. Please see the Book — "Super Unified Theory," and Book of Truth (VI) for more details on this subject — the unified force equation.

Book of Truth (IV)

Numbers, Colors, and Infinities

My son Andrew was learning to count when he was four years old. One day, he asked me how come the numbers won't stop. I was greatly surprised. The concept of infinity is in the mind of a four year old kid, but all physicists ignore the existence of the infinities. When a physics equation diverges to infinity, physicists always get rid of the part of the equation, which causes the divergence. They call this a "renormalization" process. If any theory cannot be renormalized, then it is meaningless. What can happen if the truth lies inside the part that was thrown away by those physicists? Can you imagine that a crime detector who is afraid of blood ignores all blood stains when he investigates all criminal cases?

II

There are two very important phenomena that can be understood by every ten-year old kid but are ignored by all physicists.

The first concept is "death." Why must all lives die?

The second concept is "self." What is "self?" Where did it come from?

The concept of "self" is understood by all lives. For example, when a piece of green sponge and a piece of red sponge were smashed and put into a water tank together, after a while, the green sponge cells will congregate into the green sponge ball, and the red cells also will get together with their own kind. Surprisingly, an eyeless, brainless sponge cell is able to identify its own kind.

These kinds of subjects are beyond the scope of traditional physics. A true theory should be the theory of everything. I have pointed out seven color dimensions for lives and seven color dimensions for elementary physics, but I have not unified these two sets of color dimensions yet. We need to understand that underlying meaning of those colors. Obviously, physicists have failed even to begin to tackle this problem. "Physics discusses only those aspects of world which seem free from detailed divine intervention," said those stiff-necked physicists. Fortunately, we are able to find our answers from mathematics. There are three divine concepts embedded in the number system.

The first subject that comes to my mind is how to transform the infinite to the finite. At the big bang stage, the mass density in the fire ball is infinitely high, and the temperature of the fire ball is also infinitely high. How can these infinities be transformed into finite values?

One best way to tackle this problem is by trying to create "infinity" from "finite." I am going to use a moving egg process to demonstrate this point.

Here, I have two baskets. One basket is on my left hand side, and it contains two types of eggs — red eggs and green eggs; one billion of each of them. The other basket is on my right hand side, and it is empty. My task is to move all eggs from the left basket into the right basket by observing some weird rules.
Rule 1: I can move a green egg from left to right without any penalty.
Rule 2: If I move a red egg from left to right, then I have to move one billion green eggs from right to left.

So, I begin with moving one billion green eggs from left to right. Finally, I run out of green eggs, and I have to begin to move red eggs. After the first red egg is moved from left to right, I have to move one billion green eggs back to left from right.

This task seems to be gigantic, but it will be done in a finite number of steps nonetheless. I can add blue eggs in the left basket and apply the rule 2 to green and blue eggs. This additional egg class in the egg hierarchy will make my task billions times more difficult, but it can still be done in a finite number of steps.

There are only two possible ways to create "infinity" from this process. The first method is to increase the number of different egg colors (classes in the egg hierachy) to infinity. The second way is by changing the penalty from one billion to infinity. Neither method creates "infinity" from "finite." "Infinity" is a "self," and it cannot be created from finite. "Self" is an item that cannot be derived from anything else other than itself. For example, God is a "self," a supreme Self.

III

Can you derive "infinity" from "finite?" In mathematics, two kinds of infinity are discovered and recognized. One of them is called countable infinity, and the other is called uncountable infinity. Countable infinity is a "limit point" of the countable number, such as 1, 2, 3, . . . , countable infinity. But, this "limit point" can never be reached with finite steps; it can only be reached with infinite steps. Again, we find that "infinity" is a "self."

Surprisingly, the infinity does have some "finite" characteristics. There is an infinite amount of numbers between 1 to infinity, but we are able to squeeze all those numbers into a finite space, which is the length from 0 to 1. Believe it or not, the amount of "numbers" between 0 to 1 is equal to the amount of "numbers" from 1 to infinity. This point can be proved very easily. If every number that belongs to one set can always find a corresponding number from the other set, and vice versa, then these two sets are equal. I am going to prove that the set of 0 to 1 equals to the set of 1 to infinity with three points. Two of them are end points, and the third one is an arbitrary point lying in-between the ends.

First, "1" corresponds to "1."

Second, "infinity" corresponds to 0 which equals to "1" divided by "infinity."

Finally, for any point, named N, lying between "1" and "infinity," we can always find a corresponding point that is 1/N, lying between "0" and "1."

It is amazing that we can compress an infinite amount of number into a finite space. But, the miracle does not stop here. We are able to compress all the numbers from 1 to infinity into a "point." It is a bit difficult to prove this phenomenon with common language; therefore, I will leave it for mathematicians to do the explanation. I have, however, already achieved what I intended to demonstrate: that "infinity" is not only a self, but it is also very "soft."

We all know that 3 is larger than 3 minus 1, and one trillion is larger than one trillion minus one. All finite numbers, regardless of how large, are very rigid. The relationship of larger than or smaller than is clearly defined for finite numbers. But, the relationship of larger than will lose its meaning in the arena of "infinity." "Infinity" plus one trillion is not any larger than the "infinity" itself. We can press trillions of numbers into the "infinity," and the "infinity" will not gain any weight or size. The "infinity" is a big black hole, and it can suck everything we have with no swell or sweat.

So far, we have learned two strange characteristics of "infinity." The first characteristic is "self;" the other is "softness." At this point, we do not yet know what these two characteristics mean to our real world.

IV

The infinities are colors. We have found seven color dimensions for life and seven color dimensions for the building blocks of the universe, but we do not really know the real meaning of them. Especially, we do not yet know any "direct" connection between these two sets of color dimensions. Now, the infinities are going to provide us a bridge to connect these two sets of color dimensions.

There are many ways to represent numbers. The most familiar method is by using 10 symbols, which consist of 0, 1, 2, . . . , 9. The other popular method is the binary system, which consists of two and only two symbols, 0 and 1. In mathematics, the base 10 system and binary system are identical. In other words, a 10 symbol system does not produce any more information than a two symbol system does.

In a computer, numbers are often represented by two colors, a binary system. It is "red" when the switch is "on," and it represents "1." It is "dark" when the switch is "off," and it represents "0." So, all numbers that can be represented by base "10" system can be represented by two and only two colors.

But, can the base "10" system identify all numbers? The answer is a big "NO." There is an infinite amount of numbers, which is unable to be identified by base 10 system. The most famous example is the number "Pi" that denotes the ratio of the circumference of a circle to its diameter. Today, we have found more than one million digits for "Pi" after its decimal point, but nobody knows what it is after those known digits. All mathematicians recognize that there is an infinite amount of digits after the known one million digits. The number "Pi" cannot be identified by 10 symbols; a new symbol (or color) is needed. I call it " + " color. "Pi" is equal to 3.1415926538979 + .

Believe it or not, seven and only seven colors are needed to identify all numbers. Lives, elementary particles, and numbers need seven color dimensions to identify all members in each of their own group, and these phenomena seem to be a happy coincidence. Actually, these three sets of color dimensions are unified; they are the three sides of the same truth.

First, we need to identify what those seven colors for numbers are. The number of one-third (1/3) can be written as .3333333 . . . . If we put the decimal point of the number .333 . . . in a rocket, and let it fly to right side, then the number increases its size by a factor of 10 when the decimal point passes every digit on its right side. If this decimal point flies to the right side forever, then the number of .333 . . . will become infinitely big, and I am going to use a special symbol (.3I) to identify this huge number. The number (.3I) represented the number 33333 . . . , and it is a number derived by removing the decimal point from the number .333 . . . , which is equal to 1/3.
    Again, (3 + 1/3) is eleven times larger than 1/3 (.333 . . .), but 3 + 1/3)I has a same size as .3I. This point can be understood very easily. The number (3 + 1/3)I is equal to 33333 . . . , and .3I is also equal to 33333 . . . .

These subjects of infinity seem to be very boring, but they are very important concepts for the understanding of soul and eternity. I am going to explain the symbol "I" one more time to prevent any confusion. Any number followed by a capital letter "I" denotes an infinity, which is derived with a finite number, but its decimal point has been removed by an ever-flying rocket.

The number 1/3 is seven times larger than 1/22 that is .0454545 . . . . When the decimal points were moved to right side for 10 digits,

　　3333333333.33333333333 . . . is still larger than
　　0454545454.54545454545 . . .

Actually, the above relationship remains to be true regardless of how far the decimal points were moved to right side as long as the number of places moved is a finite number. But, what does happen if the decimal points are moved to right side with infinite digits? This is accomplished by placing these decimal points on two forever flying rockets. Then, which one is larger, (1/3)I = 3333 . . . or (1/22)I = 454545 . . . ? The answer is that they have the same size. This point is not too difficult to understand because (1/3)I and (1/22)I are both infinities; therefore, they are equal.

But, we run into a big problem now. Which number is larger, (1/3)I or (Pi)I?

(Pi)I is equal to 31415926538979323846 . . .

There is no question that (Pi)I is an infinity. But, all mathematicians tell us that (Pi)I is larger than (1/3)I. Surprise! Surprise! One infinity is larger than another infinity. This point is a bit difficult to explain, and I will leave it for mathematicians to do the explanation. We are, however, able to get some ideas of the reasons of why.

The last digit for (1/3)I, if there is any, seems to be more certain. In fact, there is no such thing as last digit for an infinity. If there is one, then it cannot be an infinity. Instead, its tail is predictable for the number of (1/3)I, and mathematicians call this tail "countable." But, the tail for (Pi)I is unpredictable. We now know one million digits for (Pi)I, and nobody can predict what the next digit is until it is found by an actual calculation, but the new tail remains to be unknown. Mathematicians call this infinity "uncountable."

Square root 2 (SQR2) is equal to 1.41421356 . . . . The tail of SQR2 is also unpredictable, but it will become predictable after we square it. Square Pi will not transform its unpredictable tail to a predictable one. Obviously (SQR2)I is a new kind of "infinity," and I call it pseudo-uncountable.

Now, three different kinds of number are identified. The first kind of numbers has a tail with countable digits. All of them share the same ghost partner — countable infinity. All of them converge (or diverge) into the same infinity when their decimal points are removed. I call this kind of number "C"-colored number because all of them have a countable tail. Their ghost partner is identified as I1-color (countable infinity). For example:

1.0 = 1.000000000000000000000 . . . 000 . . .
2.0 = 1.999999999999999999999 . . . 999 . . .

The second kind of numbers has a tail with uncountable digit. All of them share the same ghost partner — uncountable infinity. These numbers can be identified by "+"-color. The uncountable infinity is identified as I3-color. For example:

Pi = 3.1415926538979323846 . . . ? . . . ? . . .

The third kind of numbers can be identified as "P"-color (its tail has a pseudo-uncountable digit). Their ghost partner is identified as I2-color. For example:

Square root 2 = 1.41421356 . . . ? . . .

In summary, every finite number has an infinite long tail, and there are three different kind of tails. The first kind of tail is predictable and countable. It corresponds to a countable infinity. I used a C-color to identify this kind of tail and an I1-color to identify the corresponding infinity. The second kind of tail is permanently unpredictable. It is marked with two "?" in above example. This tail corresponds to an uncountable infinity. I used a "+"-color to identify it and an I3-color to identify the corresponding infinity. The third kind of tail seems to be unpredictable but becomes predictable after a multiplication operation. I used a P-color to identify this tail and an I2-color to identify the corresponding infinity.

Now, we can identify all numbers with seven colors (1, c-color, p-color, + color, I1, I2, I3). For example:
0 (zero) can be obtained by using 1 divided by I3 (infinity).
2 can be obtained by using 1 + 1, and we can obtain all whole numbers with this method.
1/3 can be obtained by using .33 plus a c-colored tail, and all rational numbers can be identified with this method.

And, p-color tails are used for irrational numbers, such as square root 2; + color tails are used for irrational numbers, such as Pi.

There are three infinities, which are also numbers. They are identified by I1-color, I2-color and I3-color.

IV

Traditionally, the term of infinity carries two meanings, beyond the largest and indeterminacy. This concept is terribly misleading. As I have demonstrated, all finite numbers have an infinite tail, and all infinities are clearly defined. Infinity has three clearly understandable attributes, self, softness (indivisible) and totality (perfection). A self cannot be created by anything other than itself. But, why are there three obvious infinities, one contains others? It is seemingly contradictory, but it is not.

For example, if the entire universe is an infinity, then this universe less human can be labeled as no-man. No-man is still an infinity. Man (no-no-man) seems to be finite but is indeed carrying some attributes of infinity because the infinity is indivisible. The number "1" seems to be a finite number but it is really a "no-no-1," and the "no-1" is an infinity less 1.

All sciences, except mathematics, are unable to deal with the conception of infinity. Mathematics does accept infinities as only an abstract concept but cannot relate them as a physical reality.

The greatest infinity is "Nothingness" by definition. It is not only a Supreme Self, a complete totality, but is also absolutely indivisible.

As I have demonstrated in Book of Truth (II), all finites and infinities (the entire universe) are created from and by "Nothingness."

Again, it seems to be contradictory that the indivisible infinity, Nothingness, is able to create infinite finites, but it is not contradictory. The creation of finites or other infinities does not divide the utmost infinity, Nothingness, into pieces. All creations are permanently confined within this infinity. For every finite number, there is an infinite tail that ties it with its creator. For every life there is a soul, which is eternal, to connect it with its creator.

We are, indeed, able to analyze infinities with rules of complement. Complementary rules are the only way to deal with the concepts of permanent confinement, totality and indivisibility. We can understand these complementary rules with the principle of "example in kinds." The complementary rules for infinities are the same as the complementary rules for colors. Infinities are colors. As it is demonstrated in Book of Truth (VI), the only way to understand our basic building block in this material world is by using the concepts of color and color forces. See my book Super Unified Theory for the details of complimentary rules.

Because the infinity is indeed indivisible, it is able not only to create new infinities but also infinite finites. This indivisible principle guarantees the return of all finites to their creator. All finites are permanently confined within the infinity. Only "Nothingness," our Almighty God—the greatest infinity, is able to create infinite finites and other infinities.

Every self is immutable and unchangeable. Every self has its own soul. No other soul can ever replace yours in the past, at present or in the forever going future. Even the destruction of the entire universe can never destroy your soul. You have a soul because you are permanently confined within God.

Book of Life (III)

Soul, Eternity, and Colors

Over and over, I have discussed dimensions and colors. They are labels for labeling "things" or "events." But, they have many deeper meanings.

If I use some white powder to make a circle that encloses an automobile, then this car is trapped inside this two dimensinal circle if the driver does not want his car tires to be marked by white powder. If the driver is able to install a set of helicopter rotary blades in his car, then he will be able to lift his car into a new dimension, and he can escape the two dimensional trap by flying into the third dimension.

Obviously, dimensions have two completely contradictory meanings, traps and freedom. In sciences, the number of dimensions means the number of degrees of freedom. If the body is a four dimensional domain (three space dimensions and one time dimension), but the life has five dimensions, then there is one degree of freedom left over; therefore, the body is unable to trap the life, and the life can fly out of the body into this fifth dimension.

In Book of Life (II), I pointed out that all lives have three space dimensions, one time dimension, and seven color dimensions. But, these color dimensions in the Book of Life (II) are arbitrarily assigned by an imaginary astronaut Mr. Smith.

II

Elementary particles showed their colors by themselves through the color force interaction, and we discovered them. There is a big difference between "discover" and "assign." We should try to discover the true meaning of color dimensions for life by asking the answers from all lives.

Amazingly, all lives also can be described with four and only four colors, A, G, T, C. A is Adenine. G is Guanine. T is Thymine. C is Cytosine. A, G, T and C are four basic chemical building blocks for all lives. The human being's genes and the bacterium's genes are constructed with identical building blocks, but their nucleotide sequence is different. In other words, all lives are singing their own life song with four "universal" notes, or they are painting their self-portrait with four "universal" colors.

Remember, all "finite" numbers can be identified with four and only four colors. Fifth, sixth, and seventh colors are infinities in the number system [see Book of Truth (IV)]. Therefore, a species must possess five colors or more to ensure its survival beyond a finite time period. All individual life has four and only four colors; this is a hint that all individual life must die.

But, most of the lives have a topological donut shaped body [see Book of Life (II)], and they should possess seven colors because seven colors are needed for all topological donut to create individuality. So, there must be three more hidden colors for lives.

Many life forms have two distinguishable life generations. The jellyfish was born by a treelike creature. There is a reincarnation cycle for jellyfish. It lives one life as a treelike creature and in the next life becomes a jellyfish. So, for jellyfish, two more colors are needed, one to identify the tree jellyfish and the other for the swimming one. With these two additional colors, the jellyfish has survived for over 400 million years. As an individual, each life has four and only four colors, and every individual life must die. But, as a species, the jellyfish has six colors; therefore, it can last forever.

All bisexual species also have six colors. For a bisexual reproduction process, an ovarian cell that is "DIPLOID" has two sets of chromosomes. This ovarian cell will become a functional egg that is "HAPLOID," and it contains only one set of chromosomes. The egg actually loses half the genetical message, and it is not the same kind of life form as its producer. Believe it or not, the egg cell is actually viewed as a foreign cell by its producer. It is very clear that the first generation (haploid state) and the second generation (diploid state) are completely different life forms, and they should be labeled with two additional colors. With more than four colors, many species have survived for a long time, millions of years.

III

Many species use "virgin birth," a unisexual method for reproduction. Mathematically, unisexual reproduction could reproduce more than twice as numerous as the bisexual method for the reason that all the unisexual species deposit eggs whereas only 50 percent of the bisexual species does so. Furthermore, the unisexual reproduction method has zero risk of the possibility to waste eggs for the reason that the unification between an egg and a sperm is not always guaranteed. But, why do most of the species choose a bisexual method for reproduction? All lives survive natural selection process through a natural genetic mutation process that is very slow; therefore, the adaptability of those species is much more vulnerable than the species who choose a bisexual reproduction method. The bisexual reproduction method speeds up the mutation process in a factor of millions. The genetic mutation process is the basic process for lives to interact with the environment, and it is the beginning of intelligence. The bisexual reproduction process not only speeds up the genetic mutation process, but also speeds up the development of intelligence. The evolution process is a godsend gift indeed.

IV

Every life form with a topological donut shaped body, such as a tube feeding marine animal, should possess seven color dimensions. We have found six of them. If the life trap is ten dimensional (3 space dimensions, 1 time dimension, and 6 colors) but life itself has eleven degrees of freedom, then this life is able to escape from its trap into this freedom tunnel. But, what is this seventh color?

Many answers have been suggested. Science fiction writers call it "time tunnel;" life is able to go through this special degree of freedom into the past or future. But, the most intriguing answer was suggested by many religions; lives have souls. They can escape the ten dimensional life trap after death and enter "Heaven" or "Hell."

Which answer is right? The only way to find out is by reexamining the meanings of dimensions, colors, and the degrees of freedom.

For example, music intrinsically involves time, and there is no audience who is able to hear the second note before the first one is played. In contrast, there is no intrinsic "scanning order" built into a visual art that the eye must follow. Therefore, music is fundmentally one dimensionally, but visual art is generally two or three dimensional. But, if a picture is three million miles long, then the scanning eye has to obey an order, which is caused by our scanning ability. In fact, on cosmic scale, the visual art (multidimensional) and music (one-dimensional) are essentially the same without any difference.

It seems to be very confusing that a one dimensional object can manifest into a three dimensional monster, and a three dimensional monster can often turn into a one dimensional object. So, what shall we do here? What is right, and what is wrong?

The fact is that all of them are correct. In mathematics, for the reason of getting a unique answer, mathematicians developed a concept of "basis." A "basis" has two important meanings.

First, if an object was described with ten labels but it also can be described with three and only three new labels without losing any information, then this set with ten labels is called a reducible set. A set of labels becomes irreducible if the smaller set is unable to preserve all informations. This irreducible set is a "basis" for the system it describes. The number of labels in the basis is the "dimension" of the basis. So, the dimensions of a system are the fewest dimensions needed to describe a system, but more dimensions are allowed for describing any system.

Second, all labels in the basis have a special relationship among one another, and this special relationship is "no substitutable relationship among one another." Every label in any given basis is a "self" because it cannot be derived from any other labels. But some relationships can exist among those "selves." Surprise! Paradoxicalness! Chaos! Indeed, it is. It takes an entire special relativity theory to describe the relationship between time and space. Furthermore, colors obey complementary rule among themselves although they form a basis (11 dimensions) to represent the entire universe. For example, red plus yellow create blue, and red plus yellow and blue create colorless color. You must be confused with these statements, which seem to contradict the definition of basis. Contradiction? No! All eleven dimensions (3-space, 1-time, and 7-color) do indeed form a basis, but they will eventually return to nothingness. Every domain has life, and there is a basis to represent that life, but all will reduce into nothingness in the end.

This contradictory phenomenon can be understood easily by a simple example, an egg system. Every egg is composed with three components, egg shell, egg white and yellow yolk. These three components form a basis. Each component in this basis is a self that cannot be derived from other component or the combination of other components. They are indeed disjointed but do also have some relationships among them. They form an egg. Without any one of the components, the egg will not be an egg, a complete egg. From this example, we can easily understand what the "totality" and the "indivisibility" are. Only color complementary rules are able to analyze these attributes, totality and indivisibility.

I hate mathematical jargon, but I do not know how to get around it. Mathematics is filled with contradictory concepts. A basis is an irreducible set. Each label (or color) in the irreducible set is a "self" by definition. The irreducible basis for all number has seven colors. Three of them are infinities, and they are "self" because they cannot be derived from anything else other than themselves. These seven "self" form a one dimensional number line. But this one dimensional line can be compressed into a "point" with a value that is "0" or "nothing." How wonderful, this basis with seven irreducible colors is reduced into "one point" [see Book of Truth (IV)]. All of these definitions and logics seem to contradict one another. Fortunately, all of those contradictory concepts are correct, and they coexist together. Surprisingly, this universe began with paradoxicalness. The whole world came from "Nothing;" it remains to be "Nothing," and eventually it will go back into "Nothing."

V

In elementary particles, there are three quark colors, three generation colors and one colorless color. For lives, there are four genetic colors and two known generation colors. The third generation color is our soul. For numbers, four colors are able to identify all finite numbers. Every individual life has only four genetic colors; thus every individual life must die. The fifth color is countable infinity; it provides unlimited dimensions for a finite object [See Book of

Life (IV)]. The sixth color is a pseudo-uncountable infinity, and it is the reproduction process of a life; with this color, the species survives for millions of years while the individual life must die. The seventh color is our soul.

The unification of these three color sets is again the single most obvious self-evident evidence that there is one and only one God; therefore, one and only one utmost truth. Each color set is only the different view of the same truth. This single truth is the reason that the principle of example in kinds is valid indeed.

Now, we have unified all colors. All quarks, protons are finite objects; therefore, they can be identified with four colors (3 quark colors and one colorless color). At the point of the big bang, everything is at an infinite state; therefore, the second and third generation of quarks are needed. All necessary material or spirit for creating a life are plentifully embedded in all elementary particles. As soon as conditions were right, these seven vivid life colors will manifest into lives from those materials that were assumed to be lifeless.

God created the universe. The universe resides in God. God is an eternal road along which all beings and things walk. No Being made God, for God is a supreme Self; God is everything and nothing, and the cause and effect of all. All things originate from Him conform to Him, and at last return to Him.

There is one and only one God who resides in a "point" that is "nothing." "Nothing" is a true "Self" that cannot be made by anything else. "Nothing" is also chaos [See Book of Truth (V) — Chaos], and it is the only source of the creation. It is the home of "Eternity."

When our universe bubbled out from "nothing," a ghost partner was created at the same time.

Our universe (which includes galaxies and lives) can be described with eleven dimensions (3 space dimensions, 1 time dimension, and 7 color dimensions).

The sphere-torus (ball-donut) transformation creates life, and this is the replay of the infinite-finite transformation. All lives also should have a ghost partner, and it is our soul.

All individual life must die because it is trapped in a finite region, but this finite region can have unlimited dimensions and opportunities. This point is the subject in the Book of Life (IV). However, all life species are able to go into the infinite region because it does possess the sixth color, which represents the pseudo-uncountable infinity. The seventh color that is our soul is the true uncountable infinity, and only our soul is able to reach the Eternity.

VI

Science excludes the subjects of soul and eternity in its domain; therefore, God excludes scientists from knowing the truth. Scientists are persons who have eyes but cannot see, who have ears but cannot hear, who have brains but cannot understand the simple truth. It is very annoying indeed to hear someone denounce religions or the existence of the soul by quoting scientific logic. Most of those people do not know what science is in the first place; if they did, they would surely keep their stupidity to themselves. Furthermore, the traditional science is simply not equipped to reach the region of the utmost truth. Science is domain-bonded; it can only reveal limited truths.

In the traditional dogma, there are two distinctive meanings for eternity, an endless motion (succession) of time and an endless stillness of time. These two concepts are fuzzy, not clearly defined, and troublesome. If eternity is an endless motion of time, then where is the beginning. Also, God Himself cannot be eternal by this definition because God exists before the beginning. If eternity is an endless stillness of time, then there is no beginning nor an end. This notion denies the conception of time itself. This eternity does not exist at an infinite future but now, in the past, and in the future.

Aquinas wrote, "Even supposing that the world always was, it would not be equal to God in eternity, for the divine being is all being simultaneously without succession, but with the world it is otherwise."

All religions recognized a simple fact, the existence of soul, many thousands of years ago. There are many definitions for soul. I will discuss two traditional definitions first, then give you the true meaning of the soul at the end.

In Christianity, only human beings have soul because only human beings received breath from God. But, the meaning of soul is very vague in the whole Bible. In other words, no one is able to understand what soul is by reading the Bible. Surprisingly, the subjects of soul and eternal life are completely not related to each other in the entire Bible. No single verse in the Bible states that soul is eternal. In fact, soul can be killed or die according to the Bible.

"And fear not them which kill the body, but are not able to kill the soul: but rather fear him which is able to destroy both soul and body in hell." St. Matthew 10:28.

"Let him know, that he which converteth the sinner from the error of his way shall save a soul from death, and shall hide a multitude of sins." James 5:20.

Nonetheless, there are a few verses that discuss that the soul and the body can be preserved or saved. They do not mention how long the soul and the body can be preserved or saved.

"And the very God of peace sanctify you wholly; and I pray God your whole spirit and soul and body be preserved blameless unto the coming of our Lord Jesus Christ." 1 Thessalonians 5:23.

"But we are not of them who draw back unto perdition; but of them that believe to the saving of the soul." Hebrews 10:39.

Brahmanism describes soul in much better detail than Christianity does. In Brahmanism, soul is the true life and is eternal; the material body of a life is only a temporary shelter for the soul.

"As the embodied soul continually passes, in this body, from boyhood to youth, and then to old age, the soul similarly passes into another body at death. The self-realized soul is not bewildered by such a change." (Bhagavad-gita as it is)

Therefore, the soul is indestructible. Therefore, the soul is a Self.

"The soul can never be cut into pieces by any weapon, nor can he be burned by fire, nor moistened by water, nor withered by the wind. This individual soul is unbreakable and insoluble, and can be neither burned nor dried. He is everlasting, all-pervading, unchangeable, immovable and eternally the same. It is said that the soul is invisible, inconceivable, immutable and unchangeable. Knowing this, you should not grieve for the body." (Bhagavad-gita as it is)

VII

In the traditional tenet, the conceptions of soul and eternity are considered to be unimaginable. The acceptance of these concepts is not through understanding but with faith. Now, with understanding the attributes of infinities (Self, totality and indivisibility), we do know that the eternity is the "Nothingness," absolutely immutable — a self that neither comes to be nor passes away, nor changes, nor moves in any respect whatsoever. We also know that soul is the link between the finite material body and the eternal immutable God, Nothingness, as described in Book of Truth (IV). Soul is the seventh color of life. This seventh color is an infinity, which is eternal. All other six colors have manifested to be part of material body. Everything which exists in space-time has mass and can always be detected. This seventh color is the marker for every Self. Every self is immutable and unchangeable. Gloria, my daughter, asked me, "If you married another woman instead of Mother, would I be the same girl?" Very clearly, the answer is no. Every self has its own marker. No other marker can ever replace yours in the past, at present or in the forever going future. Even the destruction of the entire universe can never destroy your marker, which is your soul. You are a self and own your own soul forever to eternity. You have a soul because you are permanently confined within God. I understand; therefore, I worship.

UNIVERSITY OF CENTRAL FLORIDA

DEPARTMENT OF PHYSICS

ORLANDO, FLORIDA 32816-0993 (305) 275-2325

December 5, 1986

Dr. Jeh-Tween Gong
P.O. Box 1753
Bristol, VA 24203

Dear Dr. Gong:

The draft of your paper on color forces, particle decay, and QED has reached me and I found it very interesting. If you are going to be in Florida anytime soon, I would be interested in meeting you and discussing your ideas further.

Sincerely,

Ralph A. Llewellyn
Professor

RAL:lh

Book of Life (IV)

Diversification, Freedom, and Civilization

"Finite" is unlimited. A finite number can be larger than any number you can ever imagine. There is, however, a giant canyon between finite and infinity, and "finite" is absolutely unable to jump over this huge canyon to reach the bank of infinity. On the other hand, the difference between finite and infinity seems to be thinner than a hair because finite is unlimited.

If you select a big number, such as one trillion, I can always find a finite number that is bigger than your selection. Actually, nobody is able to find the boundary for finite numbers; finite is unbounded. Unlimited number of dimensions (degrees of freedom) can embed in every finite region or object. This unlimited degree of freedom for every life have created an unlimited variety of life forms.

II

Every life is trapped in two finite regions. The big trap is the environment. The second trap is its own body. For most of the lives, a donut shaped mass separates a finite region into two domains. One domain contains mass. The second domain is a "connected" space, and this domain is further separated into two subdomains. The first subdomain is a huge space, and we call it — environment. The second subdomain is part of the internal organ of a life; every creature uses this subdomain to absorb energy from the environment. So, every life is "embedded" in the environment. Every creature interacts with the environment with two surface areas. Surprisingly, most of the creatures use the outer surface to protect themselves from environment, but they use the inner surface to interact (exchange material and energy; absorb nutrition and discharge the waste) with the environment. Remember, the outer space (environment) and the inner space (surrounded by internal organs) are

"connected," and this inner space is actually a part of a large environment. But, most of the creatures have robbed the inner part
of the environment to become part of its own body, and they carry
part of the environment inside their body all the time. Each creature
is a "self," but every "self" is "nailed" down into the environment
by its own gut. Every "self" is permanently confined in the
environment.

<h1 style="text-align:center">III</h1>

Because of the imprisonment situation of all lives, they all are
struggling for freedom. The first breakthrough is the evolution of
devoloping the nerve cells. With nerve cells, a life is able to interact
with the environment in its favor, avoiding dangers and catching prey.

There are two very important breakthrough by some of those
nerve cells. One group chooses a passive method by "receiving" the
lights that are reflected by the environment, and the optical organ
has evolved from normal cells to specialized nerve cells. The other
group chooses an aggressive method by "emitting" the ultrasonic sound
to detect the surroundings, such as the echo location method employed
by many bats. Both methods have created a new degree of freedom.
Both of them enable those lives to extend their interaction with
the environment much beyond the reach of their body. They have
successfully escaped from the trap of their own body to some degrees.
Many new dimensions and degrees of freedom were created by many
lives. Many lives conquered land. Many species become the lords
of the air. The unlimited diversification of life forms is possible because
"finite" is unbounded and unlimited.

The genetic mutation is the basic mechanism of innovation and
creativity of all lives. The godsend gift of bisexual reproduction speeds
up this evolutionary process million of times faster than the virgin
birth reproduction method does. Nevertheless, for hundreds of millions
of years, the environment has had the upper hand, and all lives
have been prisoners of the environment regardless of their struggles
for creating many new dimensions and new freedom. All lives were
essentially equal in the eyes of the environment, but this situation
was changed permanently when one creature discovered a way to
control the environment.

IV

When agriculture was invented, the human race became the first creature able to "control" his own environment, and he has created many new dimensions and degrees of freedom. After the invention of language and the printing press, the mathematical law of exponential compounding speeded up the process of creating new dimensions. Air planes enabled the wingless human to fly. Televisions enabled us instantaneously to see events thousands miles away while these events are happening. The VCR even creates time; we are not only able to move the morning show to afternoon, but are also able to create time by getting rid of unwanted information by fast forwarding the VCR tape. Automatic home appliances free us from many physical labors. Computers free us from many mental labors. There are many, many more examples.

No individual human being is able to absorb all information or knowledge after the human knowledge has been exponentially compounded for thousands of years. The ways of getting around this problem are by cooperation and specialization that are the strategies invented by many creatures, such as the development of organs. So, human society as a whole is actually a super organism, and it is sad that discrimination between human races is still deeply rooted in many cultures.

With unlimited degrees of freedom, the human being is still the prisoner of the environment. Our power to control the environment has severely endangered the balance of the environment, which is still part of our own gut. The only way for life to obtain the infinite freedom is by eliminating its mass body when its soul is unified with its ghost partner. In Christian religion, this condition can only be reached after death. In Buddhism, this condition can be reached with endless meditation, and Buddha called it "Nirvana." (See Books of Religions.)

V

Vision, hearing, radar, the air plane and television are all scientific instruments; all of them have a finite capability. All these dimensions or degrees of freedom are a subset of the finite colors. None of these instruments is able to probe the region of infinity. Even with an unlimited number of instruments, we are still unable to reach the region of infinity. Actually, we are unable to put "infinity" in any laboratory because all laboratories are composed of instruments, which have a finite capability. In other words, science is unable to study any subject that is associated with infinity. God is the utmost infinity. Souls reside in God. "The question of God is outside the realm of physical experiments," said those stiff-necked physicists. This is absolutely correct indeed.

Finite can never become infinity, but finite comes from infinity. Finite is permanently confined in infinity. Moral science deals the laws of freedom. It is still in the domain of finite region but has unlimited degrees of freedom. That is the reason that traditional science is unable to tackle moral problems. Physical science is not only unable to reach the region of infinity but also any finite with unlimited degrees of freedom. Therefore, there is no hope of any kind remaining for the traditional science. The final verdict is that the traditional science is unable to understand the utmost truth, the supreme infinity. We need a new religion and a new science, a unified religion that studies infinities, souls, eternity, and that worships God. We need to construct a new civilization.

VI

The human being is especially blessed by God. We do have unlimited degrees of freedom, which is much more than all the freedom of all other creatures put together. We become an invincible ruler on the planet earth. All these achievements are the results of two weaknesses that handicapped our ancestors.

Our ancestors were unable to hunt by their running ability; they were slow runners. They were also unable to kill with their dull teeth; they had vegetarian's teeth. Their inherent handicaps forced them to invent two skills, tool making and language communication for team work.

Our ancestors also had two animal characteristics. First, the human being is the cruelest killer. Most species of hunters kill for survival. But, the human being is the only creature who enjoys killing as entertainment, such as bullfights in Spain. Matadors are still viewed as heroes today. Furthermore, human beings are the only creatures who kill one another in gigantic numbers, millions. In order to lessen the killing, a few civilizations have been created to confine this animal characteristic.

Second, the human being is one of a very few animals who have a non-restricted breeding season, and love making is more for pleasure than for the purpose of reproduction. In order to secure a mate, a civilized arrangement is necessary.

Two types of civilization have been developed to confine these animal characteristics. Western civilization does not denounce these two animal characteristics as immoral, but builds a cage to confine them. This cage is law. So, a nude painting is an art when it is placed in a cathedral, such as the Sistine chapel, because it displays the beauty of God's creation. But, it is pornography if the purpose of the picture is to stimulate sexual desire. Furthermore, bullfighting and boxing are now very civilized sports. On the contrary, the Chinese view these as non-human characteristics which should be suppressed in civilized society. Human beings should suppress these desires by elevating the human consciousness, which can only be purified and strengthened by self-discipline and meditation. The western culture established civilization with external laws, civil laws and religious laws. The eastern culture established civilization with self consciousness and internal enlightenment.

Confucius remarked, "If you regulate people by laws, they will try to keep out of jail, but will have no sense of honor. If, on the other hand, one regulates the people by morals, they will have a sense of honor and will reach out toward the good."

VII

Nonetheless, both civilizations have failed many times. Not only are Egyptian civilization and Babylonian civilization extinct, but we also have many recent failures. Nazism was born in western civilization, and it resulted in a holocaust. The Japanese warlords grew up in eastern culture, but they executed the Nunking massacre. In summary, both civilizations have failed to confine our animal instinct. With nuclear weapons on hand, our civilization is hanging by the skin of our teeth. A new religion and culture is needed for our future. We understand; therefore, we worship.

Before this book — Truth, Faith and Life — was written, the origin of what is — God, man, the universe — was shrouded in a mystery we were no closer to solving than was the chronicler of Genesis, but Gong's book has changed all that. His book is much greater than all great books: "The City of God" by Saint Augustine, "The Critique of Pure Reason" by Immanuel Kant, "The Origin of Species" by Charles Darwin, etc.

— Gwendolyn Gong

Book of Truth (V)

Chaos — the tombstone of science

Most people and civilizations do not like chaos. But, chaos is the origin of the creation. Chaos is a Self that does not require to be created by others.

Many people believe in God because they see that this universe is very orderly. The sun always rises and sets. The four seasons repeat their cycles for millions of years. Therefore, they conclude that God must be out there somewhere to control all these. If anyone tries to describe God as chaos and chaos as God, those religious persons will definitely condemn this sinful individual. The truth is that God is chaos, and chaos is God. In fact, the proportion between chaos and orderliness is that chaos is the entire pyramid except the top vertex that is orderliness.

Not only do religious persons dislike chaos, but most scientists also believe that chaos is only a nuisance while the major portion of the universe is orderly. Many scientists, including Einstein, firmly believe that they could predict the future of the universe if enough data were obtained about the present universe.

Pierre Laplace, a French mathematician, said, "The present state of the system of nature is evidently a consequence of what it was in the preceding moment, and if we conceive of an intelligence which at a given instant comprehends all the relations of the entities of this universe, it could state the respective positions, motions, and general affects of all these entities at any time in the past or future."

After the uncertainty principle was discovered at the beginning of the twentieth century, many physicists began to doubt the ability of scientists to obtain precise measurement but continue to believe that the major portion of the universe is orderly. With the help of statistics and probability theory, physicists are able to make many correct predictions in a region that is filled with uncertainties. Today, almost all mathematicians still believe that strict determinism and complete predictability remain to be the nature of mathematics while physics does face some uncertainties.

The view of those traditional sciences, physics and mathematics, is definitely wrong. Chaos is the origin of the universe. Chaos is the essence of everything and every being. It is universal.

The uncertainty principle in quantum mechanics has a lot more far-reaching implications than just the inability to obtain a precise measurement. The major portion of the universe—physics, mathematics and lives—is chaotic. I will prove this point with three arguments.

II

First, all chaotic systems can be generated from a finite number of orderly inputs that have no randomness in any of either the incoming material or the operating procedures. In other words, any orderly system can become chaotic all by itself without any external random inputs. The best examples are lives that are very orderly in all senses—genetical, chemical, mental and physical—but will eventually turn into dust.

The other example is by kneading a dough, which is mixed with a small red dough and a large white one. Very obviously, the material in this system is finite and orderly—two doughs, red and white. The kneading action is also very orderly and consists of only two actions. The one is to roll out the dough with a rolling pin; the other is to fold the dough over. Now, place the red dough on the top of white one, then press it, then roll it out. The red color is then spread out. Fold the dough over and roll it out again. After only 10 steps, the small red dough will spread into hundreds of layers that are separated by white dough. This pattern of kneaded dough is the pattern of all chaotic systems. In other words, if you plot a chaotic system, any system, then you will get a picture that is similar to the pattern of the kneaded dough we just discussed above. There is no exception.

In fact, all chaotic systems, regardless of how complex they are, are constructed by repeating two actions, rolling out and folding over. It is possible to establish a method to grade the degree of chaos of a system by comparing this system with the pattern of kneaded dough. For example, if a system has a similar pattern as the kneaded dough with three cycles of rolling out and folding over, then this system has a chaotic order that is equal to 3.

These two actions, rolling out and folding over, instinctively exist in nature; they are in motion constantly. The rolling out action is described by the second law of thermodynamics. It says that all systems are going from orderliness to chaos constantly. For example, a cup of hot tea will always cool down unless external heat is added. A drop of ink will forever disperse after it is dropped in a cup of water. Even a pyramid will eventually turn into dust. Moreover, this rolling out action is also the most powerful amplifier. It can spread a small signal or error into a large space. Therefore, a small initial uncertainty will become a chaotic monster in a short period. This rolling out amplification effect is a forever going process. Consequently, any precise scientific prediction is intrinsically impossible. The fallacy of traditional science is instinctive.

III

The rolling out action creates chaos from time; it is a slow process. The folding over action is much more dramatic; it brings far apart information or errors together into a small region. Actually, it creates symmetry. The higher the degrees of symmetry, the higher the degrees of chaos. For example, a square plug can only go into the same size square hole in four different ways. A pentagonal plug can go into its mating hole in five ways. A round plug can go into its mating hole infinite way. The higher degrees of symmetry create higher degrees of freedom, which are, in fact, chaos. "Nothingness" has the highest degree of symmetry, and it is the highest chaos.

I went to first grade when I was five years old. I was absolutely unable to learn the concept of right and left. It simply did not make sense that my right hand and teacher's left hand pointed in the same direction. I was forced to learn that my right hand is the one that holds the pencil. I finally accepted it as a school rule but not a natural law. The lack of definite direction in this entire universe is a most chaotic phenomenon indeed.

There is almost no right or left in nature. This can be understood easily with a thought-experiment. Just pretend that you receive a phone call from a Martian. After some efforts, you are able to communicate to him with a coded language. After sending him a family portrait, you tell him that the lady on the right in the picture is your wife, your daughter on the left. But, he does not know what is right or left. After many failing attempts, you thought that the

physics law is valid universally; therefore, there should be a definition for right or left in physics. So, you told him that the spinning
direction of an electron is "right." Unfortunatley, Martians are made
of anti-matter, and their electron (positron) is spinning in the left
direction. There is no way that you can tell your Martian friend
who is your wife and who is your daughter by using the terms
of right and left before the discovery of the parity non-conservation
phenomenon in Beta decay. Beta decay is the one of a very few
phenomena that are able to distinguish what is right or left in nature.
In fact, 99.99% of nature is directionless. All modern physics
theories — QED, QCD and electroweak — are described by essentially
the same mathematical structure, symmetry.

Indeed, it is very easy to see how the folding action can create
symmetry and chaos. Cut a strip of paper one inch wide and eleven
or more inches long, then make arrow marks on one side of the
paper to point to the right side. So far, there is no confusion; the
right side stays to the right regardless of where you put this strip.
Now, if you join the ends of this strip with one right side mating
with the left side (folding over action), then mark all arrows over
again. You will soon find out that some right arrows point to the
left while you have marked right arrows continuously without any
interruption. For this strip, there is no right or left. This is a very
simple experiment, and you can try for yourself.

Moreover, any cylindrical can or spherical ball can be cut into
two disjointed halves if we cut it open along the center line. But,
you cannot cut the above strip into two disjointed halves by cutting
it along the center line. Try it! This phenomenon has a very significant meaning. This strip is imbedded in any donut shaped object.
All lives have a donut shaped structure, and all lives are nailed
down into the environment. Therefore, there is no way to pull any
life out of its environment by any way of cutting except by cutting
the throat.

So, the highest degree of chaos is both directionless and perfect
symmetry. This chaos is a Self. Orderliness is the result of a symmetry breaking. Indeed, this is the case in all physics laws. The
intricate nature of our universe is chaos. Many philosophers said,
"I love orderliness and despise chaos; this world is very orderly with
many symmetries."

Berkley wrote, "If we attentively consider the constant regulari-
ty, order, and concatenation of natural things, the surprising
magnificence, beauty, and perfection of the larger, and the exquisite

contrivance of the smaller parts of the creation, together with the exact harmony and correspondence of the whole, but, above all, the never enough admired laws of pain and pleasure, and the instincts of natural inclinations, appetites, and passions of animals; I say if we consider all these things, and at the same time attend to the meaning and import of the attributes, one, eternal, infinitely wise, good, and perfect, we shall clearly perceive that they belong to the . . . Spirit, who 'works all in all,' and by whom all things consist . . . . We may even assert that the existence of God is far more evidently perceived than the existence of men."

They obviously do not know the meaning of these two words, symmetry and chaos, that the perfect symmetry is the most chaotic. The "Nothingness," our Almighty God, is the perfect symmetry and the utmost chaos.

IV

Today, many mathematicians remain to be believers in absolute determinism in the subject of mathematics. They claim that the physical world is uncertain but the mathematical world is absolute. This notion is not only stupid but sinful.

Most mathematicians believe that any mathematical system can be described with a set of finite numbers of definitions and axioms. I hate this sinful view. Five years ago, I wrote a letter to my elder brother, Hu Chen-Ming who is a very prominent mathematician, to discuss this axioms issue.

I wrote, "Indeed, modern mathematics has contributed much new knowledge to mankind, but its philosophy is absolutely wrong nonetheless. Every number is the same as a human being who has a lifestory to tell. We are able to identify any individual with a social security number, but this kind of treatment for a human being is really an insult to his human dignity. We also can identify him with a passport, including a photo, name, age, weight, height and eye color. This passport approach is similar to modern mathematics, which identifies all numbers with a few axioms. The truth is that we are unable to describe anyone's life story even with one-million word biography. Even when a video camera follows him from birth to death without any second of elapse, 99% of his life story will still be lost. Furthermore, there is a big universe inside his head that we are unable to record by a video camera.

"On the same token, every number has a chaotic tail. No one is able to find out what is the end of the tail of square root 2. All numbers have a chaotic nature, and this nature is the mirror image of the physical world. You and those stiff-necked mathematicians should know that there is one and only one God; therefore, one and only one truth is created. Mathematics is not the tools for physicists to use to describe nature, but mathematics and physics are two sides of the same coin. The physical world is chaotic and uncertain, so is mathematics."

There are many evidences of the chaotic nature of mathematics. For example, there is no rule to locate all prime numbers. The prime numbers appear in a very chaotic fashion.

The chaotic nature of numbers is also the foundation of the Famat theorem. This theorem describes a special excommunication phenomenon in the number system. For a special group of members, the result of the addition between any two members will be excommunicated from the group. For example, the numbers 64 (4 cube) and 216 (6 cube) are members of a cube group that are derived from cubed whole numbers, such as:

Whole number	Cube number
1	1
2	8
3	27
4	64
5	125
6	216
7	343
8	512
9	729
10	1000

And, 64 + 216 that is 280 will not be a member of this group. The Famat theorem says that the sum of any two such members will not remain to be their own kind for any cube group or groups of a higher order.

Three hundred years after Famat announced his theorem, it remains to be unproved because all mathematicians try to prove it with their stupid passport (axioms) methodology.

In fact, this theorem can be proved very easily by recognizing the chaotic nature of numbers.

First, arbitrarily choose a group, such as cube group – 1, 8, 27, 64, ...

Then, select two whole numbers, x and y, such as 4 and 6. Let w = x + y. It is very easy to prove that x cube plus y cube is not a member of the cube group by a simple calculation.

Now, we need to prove two points in order to prove the Famat theorem.

1) It is true for all known cases. Thousands or more cases were verified to be true and more can be done also.

2) There is no rule violator in the region that has not yet checked.

I can guarantee that there is no theorem violator in the unknown region very easily by doing some probability calculation. In fact, the probability of a theorem violator existing in an unknown region can be easily proved to be a million times smaller than the probability, which is zero in the known region.

For example, 64 (4 cube) + 216 (6 cube) = 280
    And, 4 + 6 = 10

It is very easy to find out that 280 is not a member of cube group. I have found out that the true probability for 280 to be a cube member is zero, but its theoretical probability is 1% maximum. This calculation is done by comparing two subgroups. The one is the winner set, which is composed of 10 cubed numbers in this case. The other is the ticket set that consists of all possible winning numbers; in this case, there are 1000 such numbers. The theoretical chance to be a winner is 10 winners over 1000 numbers, and it is 1%. But, 280 does not fall in the winner set. In fact, thousands of combinations have been checked out and found to be all losers.

The probability of finding a Famat theorem violator in the unknown region decrease dramatically when we push the known region into a large number and into a higher order group. For example, the probability for 9000 cube plus 1000 cube to be a violator is one out of 100 million.

It is very easy to prove that the probabilities of Famat theorem violators converge to zero. Now, I have proved the Famat theorem with two steps.

First, in any finite region, the probability for any violator can be physically verified.

Second, the probability becomes zero when we approach the infinite region.

Indeed, the Famat phenomenon is the result of the chaotic nature of mathematics.

Mathematics is not different from the physical world. It is neither more absolute nor more orderly. It is the mirror image of the physical world that is composed mainly of paradoxicalness and chaos. There is, nevertheless, a little orderliness that is manifested from the symmetry breaking, the transformation of "Nothing-Something-Ghost partner."

V

The very tiny symmetry breaking, which is observed in Beta decay, creates the material universe that displays itself in some orderly fashion. The ability to transform a disc area into a square that has the same area through the Archimede's spiral creates some orderliness in mathematics. These processes reduce infinity to finite. Our material universe is manifested from these two small windows, symmetry breaking and infinite to finite transformation. But, the instinctive natures of nature are paradoxicalness, chaos and infinities. The visible universe is only a very small portion of the entire cosmos. So far, both physics and mathematics are very successful in this visible universe, which is finite and orderly. In this visible universe, sciences have successfully found some order by reducing a large system to a smaller system that is able to be handled and analyzed, then sum those results together to represent the entire system. But, this reduction methodology is no longer valid in a region that is filled with chaos. The spirit of the universe, which is 99% of the entire universe, is invisible, immaterial, immutable, and cannot be reduced to a smaller system because its natures are infinite, chaotic and paradoxical. Therefore, the fallacy of the methodology and philosophy of both mathematics and physics are instincitve and fundamental.

Taoism and Buddhism firmly believe that the spirit of the universe is imbedded in human life, and it can be understood by an endless inward searching, mainly with the method of meditation. In a trance state, the human spirit is able to unify with the spirit of the universe. Many phenomena — such as walking on fire, chi-kong and acupuncture which are viewed as superstitions by western scientists — are the true achievements of human knowledge. The truly stupid and ignorant persons are the scientists who deny all truths that are above their heads.

Traditional science is domain-bonded, and it simply cannot reach the spirit of the universe. Traditional religions are also unable to reach the true spirit of the utmost truth because they are trapped in their empty truth. A new knowledge and methodology, a unification between science and religion, is needed to understand this utmost truth, God and His creation.

Because there is one and only one God, there is one and only one truth. The methodology of "example in kinds" is, therefore, valid. The color system in numbers is the same color system in physics. The color system in physics is the same color system in lives. With this principle, example in kinds, we are able to probe the region of immaterial and immutable, which is 99% of the true world. Furthermore, we will finally unify chaos and orderliness (See Book of God). We understand; therefore, we worship.

Buddha showed us God by denying and denouncing the knowledge, logic and even God Himself. For Buddha, the denial is the most powerful way of confirmation. Jesus showed us God by proclaiming that He Himself was God. His proclamation cannot be proved or disproved by reasoning; it has to be accepted with faith. Science showed us God by expelling God from the domain of science. Science finds a few facts but misses the utmost truth, the Almighty God. This book shows us God through understanding. I understand; therefore, I worship. This book brings us to a new world that has never before been reached by either reasoning or faith.

Book of Faith (II)

Confucianism, Taoism, and Buddhism

The Chinese have unifed Confuciansim, Taoism, and Buddhism into a super religion. But, this supreme harmony, created by this super religion, has driven China to become a second class nation. This supreme harmony has prevented most of the Chinese from seeking further advancement in other areas, such as science, democracy and public laws, for nearly two thousand years.

II

This super religion is led by Confuciansim. Confuciansim connected human being and God through a political system, headed by emperors who were sons of Heaven. This kind of connection was most favorable for all the ruling monarchs. There was no direct link between common folk and the transcendent God. In Confusianism, the connection between earth life and eternal life for common folk is through ancestral worship.

Ancestral worship is a most pragmatic approach to connect human life with God. They are absolutely certain that their mother gave birth to start their life. They are equally certain that their ancestors give lives to their families. There is a paradoxical question of who gave life to their first mother. This question was answered once to their first mother directly. They do not know the answer now because it has been lost over the long elapsed time. In reality, they do not need to know the answer as long as they are sure that there is an answer, which was given to their ancestors. They feel very comfortable to rely on their ancestors to deliver their wishes and respects to God.

This logic strongly implies a lively life after death even though this concept was not written out in verses in the Four Books of

Confucianism. In fact, Confucius did not deal with the issues of the origin or the end of the creation. He did not talk about any strange phenomena or any spiritual beings. Many scholars, therefore, classify Confucianism as a philosophy rather than a religion. Confucius did not found a religion, yet Confucianism is a religion. Many religious concepts were merged into Confucianism before and after Confucius. In Confucianism, the Supreme Being is Shang-Ti or Heaven: the two are used in a way as practically equivalent. Shang-Ti is a unitary Being who personalizes into two sexes, Mother earth and Father heaven. In Yi-ging, Book of Changes, these two sexes form sixty-four hexagrams that were presumed to be able to identify all variations, phenomena and events in the universe.

All Chinese do believe that their deceased ancestors are actually vividly alive in Heaven. The concept of heaven is imported from Buddhism. The connection between heaven and earth living family members is through the family temple. The family temple is the gateway to Heaven for deceased family members, and it is the shelter for them when they come back for a visit. So, every soul has to secure a spot (an ancestral tablet) in the family temple.

In China, all sons carry the family name. If a son died when he was still an infant, he has a spot in his family temple because he does carry the family name. But, a daughter is unable to go to heaven through her father's family temple if she died as an infant. Chinese resolved this problem with a ghost wedding ritual. When a deceased daughter reaches a marriage age, her parents place a red envelope with some money inside of it at a street corner. Any man or boy who picks up this envelope is the husband chosen by the lady ghost. No man in China will refuse a ghost wife for these reasons: that he is not prohibited from having an earth living wife, and he also will receive many wedding gifts and an inheritance from the parents of his ghost bride. Furthermore, he is afraid of the revenge of the spirit if he refuses the marriage. The wedding ceremony will proceed as if the bride were alive. This lady ghost will receive a family name from her husband, and she will find a spot in her husband's family temple. Finally, she is able to go to heaven. Her soul has found a home, and it ends her suffering of being homeless.

Confucianism provides two "connections" — absolute loyalty to the emperor who is the son of Heaven and worshiping of their ancestors who received lives from God and have returned to God's temple. A super rigid social order was established according to these two connections. Furthermore, Confucianism believes that human beings evolved from animals. Therefore, it is absolutely necessary to establish a civilization to "kill" the animal part of the human being. They constructed a super rigid social structure, and no single individual or small group of people is able to survive if they have violated these social orders. These social orders are constructed by five cone shaped structures. God resides on the vertex of the largest cone, also the highest. The Earth Mother resides on the vertex of second cone. The emperor resides on the vertex of third cone. The parents and teachers reside on the vertex of fourth and fifth cones accordingly. These are the Five vertical social orders. The base of the cones consists of a few concentric circles. Family reside at the innermost circle, then relatives, then friends, then strangers, then other creatures, and then lifeless matter.

Confucius said, "The duties of universal obligation are five, and the moral qualities by which they are carried out are three. The duties are those between ruler and subject, betweeen father and son, between husband and wife, between elder brother and younger, and those in the intercourse between friends. These are the five duties of universal obligation. Wisdom, compassion and courage, these are the three universally recognized moral qualities of man.

"Love of knowledge is akin to wisdom. Strenuous attention to conduct is akin to compassion. Sensitiveness to shame is akin to courage.

"When a man understands the nature and use of these three moral qualities, he will then understand how to put in order his personal conduct and character."

Human beings should love all beings and things according to the described order. If you love your friends more than your family, then a social order has been violated, and a disciplinary action is required. Therefore, public democracy was killed in the emperor's temple, and the creative energy of all youths is drained in family temples. Very often, a man does not have freedom to try out any new idea even at the age of forty or fifty as long as his parents are still living. Ancestral worship has turned into parental dictatorship. This fact is demonstrated by the following verses.

"The service which a filial son does to his parents is as follows: In his general conduct to them, he manifests the utmost reverence;

in his nourishing of them, his endeavor is to give them the utmost
pleasure; when they are ill, he feels the greatest anxiety; in mourning
for them, he exhibits every demonstration of grief; in sacrificing
to them, he displays the utmost solemnity. When a son is complete
in these five things, he may be pronounced able to serve his parents."
(Hsiao-ging, a Classic of Filial Piety)

The obedience for this rigid social order comes from the conviction among Chinese that this social order is God's law.

"The moral man's life is an exemplification of the universal
order [God's law], because he is a moral person who unceasingly
cultivates his true self or moral being. The vulgar person's life is
a contradiction of the universal order, because he is a vulgar person
who in his heart has no regard for the moral law.

"To find the central clue to our moral being which unites us
to the universal order, that indeed is the highest human attainment,"
said Confucius.

III

Taoism denies the notion that the emperor is the son of God.
Therefore, Taoism was often oppressed by ruling monarchs. On the
other hand, it becomes a spiritual heaven for those oppressed common folk. It emphasizes a non-order social order. For Taoism, any
artificial social order is not only harmful for a society, but it also
will endanger the health and life of individuals.

Tao is God's way. We shall follow Tao. But, what is God's
way? Where does Tao reside? And, how to live our life according
to Tao?

First, what is Tao? Tao is "nothing," and "something" is created
by "nothing." This concept is correct but it does not provide a functional mechanism to explain how everything actually works. This
original Taoism tried to explain what is the first creation but failed
to reach the domain of the truth. Indeed, it became a speculative
philosophy. After the first creation, Tao is the natural laws, which
can be observed from nature.

Second, where is Tao? Tao resides everywhere, in lives, in rocks,
and even in a pile of shit. Taoism and Buddhism believe that all

lives are created equal. Therefore, human being should love all creatures without any discrimination. This belief is completely different from the social order of Confucianism. One very prominent Taoist had a butterfly dream. He dreamed that he turned into a butterfly. He did not know whether he was supposed to be a butterfly or the butterfly was supposed to be him, a human being. This butterfly story becomes Taoism's key doctrine, and it opened two windows for two major religious issues. Our soul is able to escape from our skin bounded muscle body and transform into a new form according to our choice. Many Taoists at later time concentrated on meditation as a way to obtain an absolute freedom for their soul through this type of transformation. Also a new social order can be established by including all nature into our innermost life circle. Many Taoists lived in the wilderness, away from human companion but friendly with natural lives and things. Many of those Taoists made significant contributions to Chinese medicine.

Third, how to live our life according to Tao? Tao is our instinct. Our instinct came with birth, but we lost it after we received artificial information and education. Tao is also softness. The softness is stronger and more powerful than rigidness. This idea was told in a fighter chicken story. A rich man hired a very famous fighter chicken trainer to train a fighter chicken for him. Three weeks later, he asked the trainer, "Is my chicken ready to fight?" The trainer answered, "No, it is too strong now." Three weeks later, the rich man asked again. The trainer answered, "No, it is too proud now." Three more weeks later, the trainer said, "Yes, it is ready to fight. It behaves like a dead log now." In the ring, the strong and proud chickens did not find an opponent to fight with so they flew out of the ring. This rich man's chicken, therefore, won every fight.

Many kinds of martial art were developed with this principle. The most famous one is judo. Ju-means soft, and -do is Tao (way). Judo is a fighting technique to defeat the opponent by not confronting his force but by transferring it to unbalance him.

In Taoism, Tao is God, and God is Tao. Tao is nothingness. Tao is instinct. Tao is softness.

"The Tao that can be spoken is not the Eternal Tao. The Name that can be named is not the Eternal Name. Nameless, the Tao is the Source of Heaven and Earth; Named, it is the Mother of all beings. He that is free from selfish desires shall behold it in the spirit; He that is possessed by passions, in the outward form alone, and those two are one in substance, though differing in name; Depth, and the depth of depths, the entrance to all spiritual life." (Tao-te-ging, Book of Lao-tze.)

"Tao is an eternal road along which all beings and things walk. No Being made it, for it is Being itself; it is everything and nothing, and the cause and effect of all. All things originate from it, conform to it, and at last return to it. Thus Tao stands for the Absolute Deity, and all the phenomena produced by Him, and also for the good man's nature and principles."

Initially, more than 2000 years ago, Taoism was trying to penetrate the mystery of creation and existence. Its understanding is remarkably close to the divine truth even though it was derived mainly from a speculative methodology, and it did not have a detailed mechanism to explain how the creation worked. At a later time, another group of Taoists developed a very colorful religious system that does not closely relate to the initial Taoism's doctrine.

This modern Taoism contains three concepts. One, the souls of men live forever. Two, everyone accounts for all his works. Three, there is a Supreme Court to judge everyone's work. With good deeds, a man can go into the Immortal land. For any evil work, the retribution is surely declared sooner or later.

There are two kind of deities in the modern Taoism. One is the deified powers of nature, such as mountains, oceans, wind, and sky. The other is the deified men who have reached Immortal land.

Man is constantly in contact with deities and evil spirits. Everything, that we do or think of doing, is observed and recorded by the observing deities. They will then ascend to heaven and reports to the supreme ruler, Yuh-kwang Shang-Ti.

"When one's mind is directed to good, though the good be not yet done, the good spirits follow him; and when one's mind is directed to evil, though the evil be not yet done, the evil spirits follow him." (Yin-chi-wan, Book of Secret Blessings)

The punishments for any evil work or desire are very horrible, and it depends upon the severity of the crime. For lests evil crimes, the wicked souls have their bones beaten. For severe crimes, the souls will be boiled in oil.

In summary, Taoism has a superb theoretical doctrine that is one of the only two religions that nearly understood the real truth. Taoism is trying to connect human life to God with true understanding of God's way (Tao) by each individual. On the other hand, the modern Taoism is the most colorful and exciting religion in the world. It has countless deities. There is one deity for every human desire or need, such as god of riches to govern profits and losses, and god of war to prevent wars. There are also countless evil spirits. Many evil spirits are powers of nature. Also, some living things, when they have lived more than 500 years, can assume the human form. Many heart-breaking, romantic love stories about the love between man and humanized fox or snake are widely told as bed time stories in China. Many people still fantasize of meeting a beautiful fox girl or a mermaid. On the other hand, by wearing charms and mirrors, man is able to ward off these kinds of evil spirits. Man can always win the battle against evil spirits if he wants to be good. There are many good deities around him all the time. The power of charm for Taoism believers is the same as the Cross for Christians. Today, many educated persons view the modern Taoism that it filled with many superstitious legends as a pagan religion. But, all other religions do not have any more truths than the modern Taoism has. Superstition itself is not wrong or false. As long as you believe it with faith and apply its teaching in your daily life, then it can be as true as any supreme truth can be. The modern Taoism created a spiritual world that is closely interlocked with earth life. The moral and ethical standard for earth life is, therefore, established according to the rules of this spiritual world. Those superstitions and deities become as real as the earth life because they are indeed part of the earth life.

IV

Buddhism was evolved from Brahmanism. In the Books of Veda, Krsna is the creator.

"He who knows me as the unborn, as the beginningless. I am the source of everything; from Me the entire creation flows." (Bhagavad-Gita as it is.)

And, all lives are trapped in the reincarnation cycles of birth and death.

"For one who has taken his birth, death is certain; and for one who is dead, birth is certain." (Bhagavad-Gita as it is.)

This kind of eternal suffering is caused by material lust, attachments, and entanglement.

"While contemplating the objects of the senses, a person develops attachment for them. From such attachment comes lust, then anger, illusion, bewilderment of memory and loss of intelligence, and then one falls down into the material cycle of birth and death." (Bhagavad-Gita as it is.)

Actually, according to Vedic religion, the body is a temporary shelter for the eternal soul.

"The body changes, but the soul remains the same. As the embodied soul continually passes, in this body, from boyhood to youth to old age, the soul similarly passes into another body at death. Just as a person puts on new garments, giving up old ones, similarly, the soul accepts new material bodies, giving up the old and useless ones.

"The soul can never be cut into pieces by any weapon, nor can he be burned by fire, nor moistened by water, nor withered by the wind. It is said that the soul is invisible, inconceivable, immutable. Knowing this, you should not grieve for the body." (Bhagavad-Gita as it is.)

But, the soul is able to escape from the suffering of the reincarnation cycle by becoming a Brahman who is an indestructible, transcendental living entity, and his eternal nature is called "Self." The way to become a Brahman is through mediation to acquire the divine knowledge.

"Material enjoyments, which are due to contact with the material senses, are certainly sources of Misery. One whose happiness is within, who is active within, who rejoices within and is illumined within, is liberated in the Supreme. Shutting out all external sense objects, keeping the eyes and vision concentrated betweeen the two eyebrows, suspending the inward and outward breaths within the nostrils and thus controlling the mind, senses and intelligence, and the trancendentalist becomes free from desire, fear and anger." (Bhagavad-Gita as it is.)

In Brahmanism, one is often unable to become a Brahman in one life time, but the previous life's work and the divine knowledge will be carred to the new life.

"In whatever condition one quits his present body, in his next life he will attain to that state of being without fail." (Bhagavad-Gita as it is.)

Therefore, the Brahman state can be reached after many, many births of practice. This concept fits very well with the caste system. The process of soul purification and decontamination is by accumulating the divine knowledge and good deeds through many rebirths. A soul has to advance through the caste system to reach the Brahman state that is actually an extension and a part of the caste system. On the same token, a soul will be reborn into a lower caste or even into the animal world if he has done some evil things during one of his life times.

Buddhism does accept most of the Brahmanism doctrine in its theory. The Four Sacred Truths of Buddhism are:

1) The suffering — such as birth, aging, illness, and death — is universal in the world.

2) The cause for suffering is the material desire and attachments.

3) This suffering can be ended by Nirvana that is the heaven in Buddhism, a state of the extinction of the suffering, the annihilation of desire, and a salvation from to be reborn. Furthermore, Nirvana can be reached before the death of the body.

4) The way to attain Nirvana is the eightfold path.

There are three major differences between Buddhism and Brahmanism.

First, Buddha did not address the issue of the Creator, but the question of who and what God is becomes the center issue in the sect of "Zen."

Second, the heavenly state of Nirvana that is equal to the Brahman state can be reached before the death of the body in one life time, and the soul can be freed from many, many rebirths.

Third, Buddhism denounces the concept and the practice of the caste system. It does acknowledge the existence of the different intelligence levels among human beings. Not everybody is capable of understanding the supreme truth; therefore, some demigod legends are tolerated in lower level of teaching.

Buddhism and Taoism are the only two religions that are trying to seek the supreme truth through understanding. The rest of the religions provide answers through faith.

The highest knowledge of Buddhism is "Zen," which was established in China about one thousand years after Buddha. Zen is very highly philosophical, and most of the Buddhists do not understand it. There is a small difference between Zen and Tao. Taoism is trying to find out the supreme truth. Zen is trying to find out two answers: the supreme truth and the way to relief from the earthly suffering cycles, such as birth, aging, illness, and death.

With this additional requirement, Zen finds an answer that is similar to Taoism's answer but with one more dimension. Zen discovered the existence of a mirror image that is similar to the concept of ghost partner [see Book of Truth (II)]. But, there is a big difference between the mirror image and the ghost partner. The ghost partner is the companion of the real world. According to Zen, the mirror image is the real reality of the real world, and the real world that is filled with much earthly suffering is only a false impression. Zen does not discuss who created the first creators but what is the real world today. The real world today is an "emptiness." The "emptiness" is real, and the material world is only an eruptible bubble. Therefore, the true enlightenment can only be obtained by forgetting the existence of the material body and the surrounding world, and then the emptiness state of "Nirvana" can be reached.

Zen does recognize the soul and the life after death. And, the earthly enjoyment or suffering will extend into the life after death. But, all these enjoyments and sufferings are false impressions, created by a material demon that itself is false. The real peace and happiness is laid in emptiness.

Two stories help us to understand the meaning of emptiness. Zen doctrine was established by six Buddhists. The first story is how the second Buddhist understood Zen. This second Buddhist spent thirty years studying Confucianism and Taoism but remained unhappy. Confucianism and Taoism did not answer his question and did not comfort his heart. After ten more years of search, he met the first Buddhist and asked him for help. The first Buddhist told him, "Give me your heart, and I will comfort it for you." The second Buddhist was unable to take his heart out, and he realized that all of his anxiety was coming from his own heart, and there was nobody else who could comfort it for him. He finally realized that all of his sufferings were false impressions that were caused by himself. As soon as he threw away all these burdens, he was able to reach the state of emptiness, and his anxiety was gone. He reached an eternal happiness at last.

The second story is about the sixth Buddhist. He was a janitor in the school of the fifth Buddhist at the time that the fifth Buddhist was ready to retire and to choose a successor. The oldest disciple wrote a hymn trying to impress his teacher.

The hymn says:

My body is a Bo-tree. (Tree of Knowledge)
My heart is a mirror stand.
I clean them every day,
Not allowing dust to get on them.

This young janitor heard the poem. He said, "I can write a better hymn," and he did.

His hymn says:

The Bo-tree is not a tree.
The mirror is not a stand.
Nothing existing transcendentally,
Where can dust land?

With this poem, this young janitor was chosen as the successor because of his deep understanding of the meaning of Zen — emptiness.

In summary, Buddhism has a superb theoretical Zen doctrine that is one of the only two religions, which almost understand the real truth. The true nature of the universe is emptiness. The universe is created from emptiness, and God resides in emptiness. God is emptiness. Buddhism is trying to connect human life to God through the eternal happiness, which resides in emptiness. Each individual has to make this connection by himself, but most people are unable to understand the Zen doctrine. Again, many sects of Buddhism thrive on the superstitious demigod legends.

V

Confucianism, Taoism and Buddhism are based on a humane foundation. Buddhism is against killing in any form. Confucianism and Taoism do practice the ceremony of sacrifice, but the killing is more for a feast than for a religious ritual.

Although the teaching of Confucius did not throw any new light on any of the questions that have a worldwide interest, but the political institutions that were established according to his teaching ruled China for over two thousand years. The rigid social structure that was created according to his teaching still controls the daily life of all Chinese. This rigid culture has drained much of the creative energy of Chinese people.

Buddhism tries to relieve earthly suffering by understanding that those sufferings are imaginary bubbles, which can all be burst, and the state of emptiness that is the source of eternal happiness can be reached before the death of the material body. This kind of spiritual enlightenment can only be enjoyed by some gifted individuals. In general, it does not produce any material substance that is still a big part of the earth life.

Taoism tries to connect human life to God by preserving the Godsend instinct, by understanding the meaning of nothingness, and by living a life according to the principle of softness. In modern Taoism, the spiritual world is not only a world for the deceased but it is also a major part of the earth life.

Both Taoism and Buddhism try to discover the supreme truth. They have not only failed to formulate a convincing and understandable knowledge, but the religions they created either become unattractive because of their fuzzy conceptual ideas or degraded as a pagan religion because of the many superstitious rituals. They often cannot even convince some very brilliant, native born Chinese scholars.

Lin Yutang wrote, "I have returned to the Christian Church rather by an intuitive perception of my moral being, by one of those 'signals out of the deep' at which the Chinese excel. And I must make it clear that the process is not facile or easy, that I do not lightly change what I have always believed, that I have roamed in the pastures of sweet, silent thought and beheld some beautiful valleys. I have dwelt in the mansion of Confucian humanism, and climbed the peaks of Mount Tao and beheld its glories, and have had glimpses of the dissolving mist of Buddhism hanging over a terrifying void, and only after doing so have I ascended the Jungfrau of Christian belief and reached the world of sunlight above the clouds."

On the other hand, a few individuals who, without any modern knowledge, have attained a true understanding through the teaching of Taoism and Buddhism were indeed able to reach a similar understanding described in my book. The conception of emptiness or nothingness is not only a religious notion but a reality in all walks of life. Musashi, Sword Saint of Japan, discovered that the "Way of Sword" is "No Way." In the Book of Emptiness, a chapter of his book—A Book of Five Rings, he wrote, "Until you realize the true Way, whether in Buddhism or in common sense, you may think that things are correct and in order. However, if we look at things objectively, for the viewpoint of laws of the world, we see various doctrines [limited truth] departing from the true Way. Know well this spirit, and with forthrightness as the foundation and the true spirit as the Way. Enact strategy broadly, correctly and openly. Then you will come to think of things in a wide sense and, taking the emptiness as the Way, you will see the Way as emptiness. In the emptiness is virtue, and no evil. Wisdom has existence, principle has existence, the Way has existence, but spirit is nothingness."

There are some significant differences between these three religions. Their doctrines are different. Their institutions are divided. But, they were united in the heart of Chinese people. Confucianism is a dominant force among Chinese. It regulates even the manner in which Chinese shall sit, stand, and sleep. But, Chinese also seek help from Taoism or Buddhism to relieve their earthly suffering and to relieve the suffering caused by the lifetime confinement imposed by Confucianism. There are three major religions in China, but most of the Chinese public believe in all three religions at the same time even when the difference among them is great. A vivid theme described by Jeanne Larsen in her novel "Silk Road" can demonstrate the way of how Chinese have united Taoism and Buddhism.

"Now a soul arrives at the gates of the underworld. . . . It goes to judgment before Yama [Deity in Buddhism,] great king of the Realm of Darkness. Who will decide what fate it has earned by its actions in the life just gone by: perhaps a term in purgatory, to await release through the prayers of the faithful; perhaps rebirth as the lowest of beasts; perhaps an eternity of torment, . . . perhaps another human life with its feet set at last on the way to paradise. . . . Leering, the Gatekeeper conducts the soul to the tribunal of the implacable judge of the netherworld. . . . The soul approaches the bench. Yama orders the General of the Five Way to read the record of its actions in the Book of Life and Death. . . . This soul's sins, though not few, are merely venial; . . . 'And to the good?' King Yama asks. . . . King Yama nods. The story rings familiarly in his divine ears: a fortunate soul, born where it could hear the teachings of the Law, so that it had the chance to see beyond the false veil of the senses' lying signals and thus draw closer to enlightenment;

a soul choosing instead to take fiction as truth and to tread the way of the body and its flimsy delights. . . . It will not be endless torment, but the next rebirth will not be a pleasant one. . . . 'Mercy!' it cries. 'In the name of Lady Guan-Yin [Saint of Buddhism] the compassionate, . . . I beg for mercy.' . . .

"There is a disturbance at the door. . . . A young man with an old man's eyebrows . . . demanding to be let in. . . . He wears silk robes fashioned in the style worn by the Taoist Immortals of the Heaven of Upper Purity. . . . 'Permit me to introduce myself, Your Most Buddhistic Highness,' says the Taoist, bowing to the precise angle demanded by correctness, and no more. . . . 'I bring you greetings from the Ruler of the Taoist Heavens and Monarch of the Ten Thousand things. . . . I-or, well, the Jade Emperor [Taoism] has, ah, taken a special interest in the case."

Not only both Taoism and Buddhism are coexisting in a harmony, but they are indeed religions of the truth and religions of a vivid culture, which has realized that both the earth life and the scientifc realm are only a small part of a large cosmos. Together, they have created the greatest culture in the world. Together, they have created the greatest religion for the mankind.

Book of Faith (III)

Christianity

Christianity is the most powerful religion on earth today. It has broken the national boundaries, cultural boundaries, and racial boundaries. This enormous success comes from one word—faith. Christianity is a religion that does not seek the truth. There are many stories in the Bible, and all followers should believe them with faith. Anyone going into any arena outside the Bible to seek the truth was expelled immediately by churches during the Middle Ages. Science was established initially by those expelled Christians.

With faith, Christians have no need for any truth. Truth or false is irrelevant for the spiritual life. This special characteristic has made Christianity invincible from all attacks by science. On the same token, Christianity is also invincible from attacks by all cultures. The Bible is not a book of truth but a book of faith. Christianity is not a religion of truth but a religion of faith.

II

In the Old Testament, God is the Creator, but there is no clear explanation where God came from. God is a manlike being.
"So God created man in his own image, in the image of God created he him; male and female created he them." Genesis 2:27.

In the Old Testament, death was not an inevitable consequence for human being at the initial creation. It is the result of Adam's sin.
"But of the tree of the knowledge of good and evil, thou shalt not eat of it: for in the day that thou eatest thereof thou shalt surely die." Genesis 2:17.

The reproduction process of all creatures excluding human being was created at the initial creation.

"And God said, Let the earth bring forth the living creature
after his kind, cattle, and creeping thing, and beast of the earth
after his kind; and it was so." Genesis 1:24

The reproduction process for human being was not created at
the initial creation but is the result of Eve's sin. Moreover, children
not only represent sorrow but are the results of punishment from God.

"Unto the woman he said, I will greatly multiply thy sorrow
and they conception: in sorrow thou shalt bring forth children; and
thy desire shall be to thy husband, and he shall rule over thee."
Genesis 4:16.

Furthermore, Jehovah, God of the Hebrews, is a very emotional
Being. He is very jealous of any other Gods and constantly in battle
with many foreign Gods.

"Thou shalt have no other gods before me." Exodus 20:3.

"And it shall be, if thou do at all forget the LORD thy God,
and walk after other gods, and serve them, and worship them, I
testify against you this day that you shall surely perish. As the nations which the LORD destroyeth before your face, so shall ye perish;
because ye would not be obedient unto the voice of the LORD your
God." Deuteronomy 8:19-20.

"But the prophet, which shall presume to speak a word in my
name, which I have not commanded him to speak, or that shall
speak in the name of other gods, even that prophet shall die."
Deuteronomy 18:20.

He often destroyed a whole tribe because of the unfaithfulness
of those tribe men.

"And thou shalt not go aside from any of the words which
I command thee this day, to the right hand or to the left, to go
after other gods to serve them. But it shall come to pass, if thou
wilt not hearken unto the voice of the LORD thy God, to observe
to do all his commandments and his statues which I command thee
this day; that all these curses shall come upon thee, and overtake
thee." Deuteronomy 28:14-15.

"The LORD shall smite thee with a consumption, and with
a fever, and with an inflammation, and with an extreme burning,
and with the sword, and with blasting, and with mildew; and they
shall pursue thee until thou perish." Deuteronomy 28:22.

"The LORD rained upon Sodom and upon Go-mor-rah brimstone and fire from the LORD out of heaven; and he overthrew those cities, and all the plain, and all the inhabitants of the cities, and that which grew upon the ground." Genesis 19:24-25.

Jehovah has many angels. He often communicated with His people, Jews, through angels.

"And the angel of the LORD appeared unto the woman, and said unto her, Behold now, thou art barren, and bearest not: but thou shalt conceive, and bear a son." Judges 13:3.

Most of these people who were contacted by angels became prophets. But, Jehovah did also make direct contact with people many times according to the Old Testament.

"And the LORD God called unto Adam, and said unto him, where art thou?" Genesis 3:9.

"Now the LORD has said unto Abram, Get thee out of my country, and from thy kindred, and from thy father's house, unto a land that I will shew thee." Genesis 12:1.

God continuously walked with people who lived on earth even after He had driven Adam and Eve out of the garden of Eden.

"So he drove out the man; and he placed at the east of the garden of Eden Cher-u-bims, and a flaming sword which turned every way, to keep the way of the tree of life." Genesis 4:24.

"These are the generations of Noah: Noah was a just man and perfect in his generations, and Noah walked with God." Genesis 6:9.

Today, nobody is able to walk with God the same way as those prophets did. God resides only in Heaven now, and Heaven is the dwelling place of God.

"But our God is in the heavens: he hath done whatsoever he hath pleased." Psalms 115:3.

So, Heaven is a "place" according to the Bible. Again, there are three kinds of description of this place. First, Heaven is outside of the earth.

"In the beginning God created the heaven and the earth." Genesis 1:1.

Second, heaven is the city of Jerusalem.

"But ye are come unto mount si-on, and unto the city of the living God, the heavenly Jerusalem, and to an innumerable company of angels," Hebrews 12:22.

"And I saw a new heaven and a new earth: for the first heaven and the first earth were passed away; and there was no more sea. And I John saw the holy city, new Jerusalem, coming down from God out of heaven, prepared as a bride adorned for her husband." Revelation 21:1-2.

Third, Heaven is a place for the poor and the undefiled.

"Blessed are the poor in spirit: for theirs is the kingdom of heaven." St. Matthew 5:3.

"To an inheritance incorruptible, and undefiled, and that fadeth not away, reserved in heaven for you," 1 Peter 1:4.

Today, Heaven often means the place for eternal life. This kind of heaven is necessary because the death of everyone's flesh is confirmed to be inevitable.

"For if ye live after the flesh, ye shall die: but if ye through the spirit do mortify the deeds of the body, ye shall live." Romans 8:13.

At this point, a true religion emerged. The Old Testament has painted a very beautiful picture of human life. We have a God who is the creator. He is our Father. He is an emotional being just like us, having love, hatred, anger, and joy. He walked with our ancestors side by side. He spoke to many of the prophets from time to time. He ruled us with terror. But, He also often sent angels to help us. Most importantly, we can relate to Him.

III

Nevertheless, this kind of direct connection with God was lost after the crucifixion of Jesus Christ. For ordinary Jews, the only formal way to communicate to Jehovah is through sacrificial offerings. For Christian, the only way to communicate with God is by accepting Jesus Christ. The authority of Jesus Christ is based on the notion that he is the Son of God. In the Old Testament, many Jews can be sons of God. Many sons of God were recorded in Bible.

"When the morning stars sang together, and all the sons of God shouted for joy?" Job 38:7.

"But as many as received him, to them gave he power to become the sons of God, even to them that believe on his name." St. John 1:12.

In the New Testament, Jesus becomes the only Son of God or Son of Man.

"And the angel answered and said unto her, The Holy Ghost shall come upon thee, and the power of the Highest shall over-shadow thee: therefore also that holy thing which shall be born of thee shall be called the Son of God." St. Luke 1:35.

"And he said unto me, Son of man, stand upon thy feet, and I will speak unto thee." Ezekiel 2:1.

"And said, Behold, I see the heavens opened, and the Son of man standing on the right hand of God." The Acts 7:56.

From these verses, two notions incarnated: 1) Jesus is elevated to become God Himself as the Trinity doctrine suggested. 2) God is a man, an emotional, lovable and touchable man.

The reason of needing salvation from Jesus is because all men have sin. Sin is inherited, and there is no way to clean it off except with the blood of Jesus.

"Wherefore, as by one man sin entered into the world, and death by sin; and so death passed upon all men, for that all have sinned." Romans 5:12.

"He that committeth sin is of the devil; for the devil sinneth from the beginning. For this purpose the Son of God was manifested, that he might destroy the works of the devil." 1 John 3:8.

"But if we walk in the light, as he is in the light, we have fellowship one with another, and the blood of Jesus Christ his Son cleanseth us from all sin." 1 John 1:7.

Many teachings of Jesus Christ are also deviated significantly from the Old Testament, such as,

"Then said Jesus unto them, I will ask you one thing; Is it lawful on the sabbath days to do good, or to do evil? to save life, or to destroy it? And looking round about upon them all, he said unto the man, Stretch forth thy hand. And he did so: and his hand was restored whole as the others. And they were filled with madness, and communed one with another what they might do to Jesus." St. Luke 6:9-11.

"Keep the sabbath day to sanctify, as the LORD thy God hath commanded thee. Six days thou shalt labour, and do all thy work. But the seventh day is the sabbath of the LORD thy God: in it thou shalt not do any work, thou, nor thy son, nor thy daughter, nor thy manservant, nor thy maidservant, nor thine ox, nor thine ass, nor any of thy cattle, nor thy stranger that is within thy gates;

that thy manservant and thy maidservant may rest as well as thou."
Deuteronomy 5:12-14.

"And thine eye shall not pity; but life shall go for life, eye
for eye, tooth for tooth, hand for hand, foot for foot." Deuteronomy
20:21.

"Ye have heard that it hath been said, An eye for an eye, and
a tooth for a tooth: But I say unto you, That ye resist not evil:
but whosoever shall smite thee on they right cheek, turn to them
the other also." St. Matthew 5:38-39.

In summary, Jesus Christ established Christianity with three
major revolutions.

First, he made Jehovah, who was a tribe God, the God of
mankind. This was the major step for allowing Christianity to become
an international religion.

"Even us, whom he hath called, not of the Jews only, but also
of the Gentiles." Romans 9:24.

"Is he the God of the Jews only? is he not also of the Gentiles?
yes, of the Gentiles also:" Romans 3:29.

"Unto me, who am less than the least of all saints, is this grace
given, that I should preach among the Gentiles the unsearchable
riches of Christ;" Ephesians 3:8

Second, he becomes Son of God, or he becomes God. Therefore,
he is able to perfom miracle by himself. This is also the foundation
of the trinity doctrine. In the Eastern religions, live sacrifice is not
part of the religious ritual, but the sacrifice with life and blood
is a big subject discussed in the Old Testament.

"And he shall kill it on the side of the altar northward before
the LORD: and the priests, Aaron's sons, shall sprinkle his blood
round about upon the altar." Leviticus 1:11.

The crucifixion itself is not a religious ceremony, but the crucifixion of Jesus Christ become the last sacrifice for the mankind. The
crucifixion of Jesus Christ has lifted Christianity from a primitive
belief into a civilized religion.

After the crucifixion of Jesus, only the blood of Jesus is able
to wash out the sins of all Christians. Jesus has become the only
connection between human being and God in the Christian doctrine:

"Likewise reckon ye also yourselves to be dead indeed unto sin,
but alive unto God through Jesus Christ our Lord." Romans 6:11.

This connection is the entire spirit of Christianity. This connection is simple enough for all common folk to understand. Furthermore, if anyone chooses to believe in this connection with faith,

then it makes all the sense in the world. If anyone chooses not to believe in this connection, he has failed to prove that it is wrong by any means, such as traditional science, philosophy, or other religions, during the last two thousand years.

Third, he provides a very easy method of attainment to salvation. He gave human being a wonderful earth life through three words: faith, love, and hope.

With faith in him, everything becomes possible:

"And Jesus said unto them, Because of your unbelief: for verily I say unto you, If ye have faith as a grain of mustard seed, ye shall say unto this moutnain, Remove hence to yonder place; and it shall remove; and nothing shall be impossible unto you." St. Matthew 17:20.

With faith in him, he can sanctify your soul:

"To open their eyes, and to turn them from darkness to light, and from the power of Satan unto God, that they may receive forgiveness of sins, and inheritance among them which are sanctified by faith that is in me." The Acts 26:18

With faith in him, you will receive the divine love:

"For God so loved the world, that he gave his only begotten Son, that whosoever believeth in him should not perish, but have everlasting life. For God sent not his Son into the world to condemn the world; that that the world through him might be saved. He that believeth on him is not condemned: but he that believeth not is condemned already, because he hath not believed in the name of the only begotten Son of God." St. John 3:16-18.

Furthermore, you will be loved by your brethren:

"Hereby perceive we the love of God, because he laid down his life for us: and we ought to lay down our lives for the brethren." 1 John 3:16.

With faith in him, you will rejoice in hope of the glory of God:

"Therefore being justified by faith, we have peace with God through our Lord Jesus Christ: by whom also have access by faith into this grace wherein we stand, and rejoice in hope of the glory of God." Romans 5:1-2.

With faith in him, you can attain salvation without works and deeds:

"Where is boasting then: It is excluded. By what law? of works? Nay: but by the law of faith. Therefore we conclude that a man is justified by faith without the deeds of the law." Romans 3:27-28.

There are unlimited benefits by believing in the Jesus connection. The Jesus connection not only fails to provide any guidance
for moral and ethical standards but it provides a safe heaven for
all immoral behaviors; because, human "work" has an absolute zero
value for the salvation of the human soul. Even a most evil murderer
is able to go to heaven as long as he accepts Jesus Christ as his
savior before his last breath. Thus, the slave trade was as moral
as gold and silver trades. In fact, a person has no need of feeling
guilty for living with devils or demons for six days as long as he
goes to church on the seventh day to worship God through accepting
Jesus Christ. In churches, every Sunday the ministers stand and address the congregation with following words: "Almighty God, in
his mercy, has given his Son to die for us and, for his sake, forgives
us all our sins. As a called and ordained minister of the Church
of Christ, and by his authority, I therefore declare to you the entire
forgiveness of all your sins, in the name of the Father, and of the
Son, and of the Holy Spirit."

In Bible, nonetheless, there is a contradicting view concerning
the issue of works and faith:

"Even so faith, if it hath not works, is dead, being alone. Yea,
a man may say, Thou hast faith, and I have works: shew me thy
faith without thy works, and I will shew thee my faith by my works.
Thou believest that there is one God; thou doest well: the devils
also believe, and tremble. But wilt thou know, O vain man, that
faith without works is dead?" James 2:17-20.

The Christian philosophy does provide some influences for
establishing Christian moral and ethical values. But, these moral
and ethical values in the Christian civilization are developed mainly
through social needs rather than following Christian religious re-
quirements. Furthermore, these moral and ethical values have no
supervising authority. The civil laws were developed to maintain
the social order. On the contrary, the moral and ethical values in
China have very strong supervising authority; therefore, the civil
laws were underdeveloped there.

IV

The lack of supreme moral value and the existence of a safe
heaven for all evil things do allow Christian civilization to have
much more freedom and energy. On the contrary, the rigid social

order and rigid moral value have oppressed much of the useful energy in China.

The authority of the Roman Catholic Church was further weakened by many religious wars and the birth of science. This weakened Church authority allows even more freedom. And much more energy was released into the Christian civilization after Medieval time. But, most important of all, Christian civilization has acquired two special characteristics— tolerance and compromise that are virtually nonexistent in the Chinese culture. Tolerance and compromise have provided Western civilization even more freedom and energy.

Often, the cause of success is also the cause of ultimate failure. The simplicity of the Christian theology is the major reason for its success in attracting believers internationally. Christianity does not seek truths but gives answers. Christianity has tolerated science and has compromised with science for the last 500 years. This tolerance and compromise have created the greatest civilization on earth.

Today, many truths have been found and understood. Many stories in Bible become very awkward and difficult to be swallowed by many educated people. On the same token, many religious people are also unable to swallow many truths discovered by knowledge. Therefore, many religious groups refuse to send their children to public schools. Refusing to accept the truth and knowledge is the first step in murdering the lively energy of any culture.

Christianity has been challenged many times, but most of the challenges come from external sources, such as other cultures, or other religions. The challenge by science is sort of from within, but it has been dodged by compromising and avoiding the issue. With faith, the hunger for truth was easily satisfied for most of the people. For many of them, there is no truth worth discussing as a religious subject if the truth is not recorded in Bible. After all, Christianity is a culture of faith; therefore, there is no reason for arguing over the truth. Amazingly, this strategy of separating faith from truth has made Christianity invincible from attacks by sciences and cultures in the past.

The first major challenge for Christian civilization in modern times was the hippy movement. This movement tried to find a new degree of freedom to liberalize the human soul while the soul is still dwelling within a living body. They did find two tunnels, sex and drugs. The hippy movement seems to have died down, but its impact can never be removed. The reincarnation of the movement into other forms of culture is inevitable as long as Christianity continues to provide a safe heaven for all evil behaviors. Christian teaching is unable to revive the bankrupted moral values after the sexual revolution and the drug invasion. This bankrupted moral value will eventually destroy Christian civilization.

In Bible, God is a father figure with unlimited power, authority, glory, love, anger, and hatred. It is not only very easy for most of the people from all cultures to relate their problems to the Christian's God, but Jesus also provides a guaranteed safe passage way to salvation for all sins regardless of how evil they are. Christianity is the most attractive religion on earth and has created the greatest civilization on earth. But now, the simplicity of the Christian doctrine is no longer a religious driving force because most people on earth are able to understand more difficult issues, much more than ever before. The strategy of separating faith from truth is also becoming unacceptable for many people. The validity of the bare testimonies and the revelation of God should be self-evident and understandable. The origin of faith is understanding, a Godsend gift, which is not from scientific evidence nor from a proof. Understanding is the result of unifying three principles, Self-evidence principle (instinct and reasoning), hypotheses principle (interplay between theory and experiment, science), and faith (the principle of example in kinds). Faith without understanding is hypocrisy, is superstition. We understand; therefore, we worship.

Now, it is time for Christianity to merge and unify with other cultures and religions. It is time for Christianity to merge and unify with the truth, which is discussed in the Books of Truth.

Book of God

God and His manifestations

There is one and only one God. God created the universe, lives, physics laws and everything else. The entire universe flows out from God. There is no external vantage point outside of God; the entire universe resides in God. Thus God is unobservable.

God is an Infinite Self. No Being made God, for God is the only Supreme Self. He is everything and nothing. The Supreme Self is the Supreme Infinity. Nothing is able to increase the size of this Supreme Infinity. Nothing is able to reduce the size of this Supreme Infinity.

The one and the only God manifests into two Bodies, the material universe and its ghost partner. This material universe furthers its manifestation into eleven dimensions, four visible dimensions (3 space coordinates and time) and seven invisible colors. These eleven dimensions are the flesh and bones of all things and all beings. All lives flow out from these eleven dimensions. Love, anger and intelligence are the manifestations of these eleven dimensions. Monotheism and polytheism are therefore both valid.

Why must God manifest into two Bodies? God is Nothingness. Why must Nothingness transform into a material universe and a ghost partner? Nothingness is the utmost symmetry. The utmost symmetry is the utmost chaos. Therefore, only Nothingness, the utmost chaos, can shake the Nothingness into two Bodies. At the same time, the Nothingness, in fact, remains to be Nothingness in the past, at present, and in the forever going future.

The seed of life is embedded in all things, even in lifeless things. Thus, the flow of lifeless material can sustain a living life. Lives bubble out from the lifeless background, but even the entire lifeless background is indeed alive. The entire material universe is the flesh and bones of God's material Body. The ghost partner of this Body is God's Soul. God (the Supreme Nothingness), the material Body

(the material universe), and the ghost partner (unified force) con-
stitute a Trinity. All three are one. The one is three. God sowed
the seed of life in all things at the point of creation. God created
universe, lives and intelligence.

The interaction between the material universe and its ghost partner will eventually unite them, the annihilation or the big crunch.
A new universe will manifest out from the old ghost partner. This
new universe, composed of anti-matter, is the mirror image of the
last universe but has a size at least twice as big as the last one
had. The universes will double their size after each reincarnation,
the big bang and the big crunch.

All finite things and beings flow out from God, the Supreme
Infinity and Supreme Self. Each life is a self, a small self. Each
self is the manifestation of the Supreme Self. Each self is an image
of God. Each life tells its own testimony about the glories of God.
There is one and only one God, but He has manifested into infinite
forms, the beautiful creatures in the oceans, the lords in the air,
the kings of the jungles and the super organism of human society.
God is the Supreme Creator.

Darwin wrote, " . . . that He created a few original forms capable
of self-development into other and needful forms, as to believe that
He required a fresh act of creation to supply the voids caused by
the action of His laws."

II

The existence of God is self-evident. I have demonstrated this
point through out this entire book. Even in the traditional tenet,
the existence of God can be proved with a posterior proof in three
ways: from the facts of experience and the evidences of nature, from
a principle of causality — an efficient cause, and from reasoning.

Locke wrote, "From the consideration of ourselves, and what
we infallibly find in our constitution, our reason leads us to the
knowledge of this certain and evident truth — That there is an eternal,
most powerful, and most knowing Being."

Augustine wrote, "Behold, the heavens and the earth are; they
proclaim that they were created; for they change and vary . . . They
proclaim also that they made not themselves 'therefore we are, because

we have been made; we were not therefore, before we were, so as to make ourselves' . . . Thou therefore, Lord, madest them."

I understand, therefore, I worship. If you don't understand, you should worship God with faith. Taoism, Confucianism, Buddhism, and Christianity do provide a wonderful connection between God and you. They all recognize the existence of God.

"God is an eternal road along which all beings and things walk. No Being made Him, for He is Being Himself; He is everything and nothing, and the cause and effect of all. All things originate from Him conform to Him, and at last return to Him. Thus God stands for the absolute Deity, and all the phenomena produced by Him, and also for the good man's nature and principles." Taoism.

"Thus God is indestructible. Being indestructible, it is eternal. Being eternal, it is self-existent. Being self-existent, it is infinite. Being infinite, it is vast and deep. Being vast and deep, it is transcendental and intelligent. It is because it is vast and deep that it contains all existence. It is because it is transcendental and intelligent that it embraces all existence. It is because it is infinite and eternal that it fulfills or perfects all existence." Confucianism.

"As in the great sky the wind is blowing everywhere, so all the cosmic manifestation is situated in Me. The whole cosmic order is under Me. By My will it is manifested again and again, and by My will it is annihilated at the end. Although I am unborn and My transcendental body never deteriorates, and although I am the Lord of all sentient beings, I still appear in every millennium in My original transcendental form. And when you have thus learned the truth, you will know that all living beings are but part of Me — and that they are in Me, and are Mine." Brahmanism.

"In the beginning God created the heaven and the earth, And the earth was without form, and void; and darkness was upon the face of the deep. And the Spirit of God moved upon the face of the waters. And God said, Let there be light: and there was light. And God saw the light, that it was good: and God divided the light from the darkness. And God called the light Day, and the darkness he called Night. And the evening and the morning were the first day." Genesis 1:1-5.

"The question of God is outside the realm of physical experiments. Any experiment needs to have control and variable parts. God cannot be excluded from either of these. Science discusses those aspects of the world which seem free from detailed divine intervention," said many scientists. Traditional science excludes God from its domain; thus, science is denied of knowing the utmost truth. Even idiots worship God through idols. Even idiots know more truths than those stiff-necked scientists. Idolatry is not a smart thing to do but is a perfect valid "Way" for those who cannot comprehend the existence, the nature, the attributes of God. God is immaterial, immutable, and invisible. Therefore, to use an image for allowing common folk to sense the existence of God, to understand God's attributes and essence is indeed valid and noble. In fact idolatry is deeply imbedded in every religion, Christianity, Taoism, and Buddhism. Christianity is against image worship for other false gods, but the statues of Virgin Mary, Jesus Christ and Cross are in every Catholic cathedral; even the statues of many saints are also displayed in many chapels. Both Taoism and Buddhism are deeply convinced that not only any image or idol is false, but the entire material universe is also only a bubble that is waiting its turn to bust, but they both still allow the statues of True Man and Buddha in their temples. Idolatry creates not only legends also cultures, many vivid cultures.

Pascal was not very versed on the subjects of faith and God, but his reasoning is still a great wisdom for those ignorant scientists.

Pascal wrote, "Which will you choose then [God or no God]? Let us see. Since you must choose, let us see which interests you least. You have two things to lose, the true and the good; and two things to stake, your reason and your will [what are they and where do they come from?], your knowledge and your happiness; and your nature has two things to shun, error and misery. Your reason is no more shocked in choosing one rather than another, since you must of necessity choose. This is one point settled. But your happiness? Let us weigh the gain and the loss in wagering that God is. Let us estimate these two chances. If you gain, you gain all, if you lose, you lose nothing. Wager then, without hesitation, that He is." This is indeed a stupid way to create faith, but it is still much better than no faith.

III

God is the infinite perfection. "Why is there evil then if God is the infinite perfection? Since everything that happens is within God's power, which is omnipotent, how can we account for the sin of Satan or the fall of man?" asked many people, Christians, pagans, or atheists.

The infinite perfection is indivisible. Being indivisible, there is no goodness, nor evil. Only in the finite region, the imperfection appears. Only in the finite region, evil is separated from goodness. Goodness and evil both reside in the finite region. They are judged by human desires and pleasures that are both fuzzy concepts. The goodness of God is no way measured by human desires and pleasures. The goodness and the evil on earth are not God's creation but ours.

Montaigne wrote, "That the taste for good and evil depends in good part upon the opinion we have of them. . . . If evils have no admission into us, but by the judgment we ourselves make of them, it should seem that it is, then, in our power to despise them or to turn them to good. . . . If what we call evil and torment is neither evil nor torment of itself, but only that our fancy gives it that quality, it is in us to change it."

Socrates wrote, "No man voluntarily pursues evil, or that which he thinks to be evil. To prefer evil to good is not in human nature; and when a man is compelled to choose one of two evils, no one will choose the greater when he may have the less."

In reality, goodness and evil are defined by "force." To place a bomb in a civilian airliner by those weak and oppressed people is called terrorism, the greatest evil. But, to bomb a small nation's capitol with hundreds of bombers, resulting in hundreds of innocent civilian causalities, can be proclaimed as moral actions, operations just cause.

Spinoza wrote, "God and evil indicate nothing positive in things considered in themselves, nor are they anything else modes of thought . . . One and the same thing may at the same time be both good and evil or indifferent . . . There is nothing which by universal consent is good or evil, since everyone in a natural state consults only his own profit."

Because both goodness and evil are finite subjects, they are subjected for changes. The fact is that no one nation can be a super power forever. There were Egyptian civilization, Babylonian civilization, Roman Empire, Arab Empire, Ottoman Empire, then Spanish century, then British century, then American century, and now is the beginning of Pacific century. The judgement for goodness and evil will definitely be in the hands of Eastern culture for this coming century.

Sun Tzu, the War Saint of China, wrote, "For to win one hundred victories in one hundred battles is not the acme of skill. To subdue the enemy without fighting is the acme of skill. Thus, what is of supreme importance in war is to destroy enemy's will and plan; next best is to disrupt his alliances; next best is to destroy his army; the worst is to attack cities."

Many direct military interventions in Vietnam, Libya, Afghanistan, Lebanon, Grenada and Panama in the recent years are direct proofs that the down fall of the super powers is inevitable.

Furthermore, there is indeed an absolute goodness that is infinitely above the earthly goodness. In fact, the rotation of power is God's way to award the goodness and to assure the retribution for evil.

Only when all men worship this absolute goodness and establish a universal civilization according to this absolute goodness, although nations can still exist, men can then decide what is truly good and what is truly evil. Then, there will be only goodness, no evil. This absolute goodness is the infinite intellect, the infinite righteousness, and the infinite love and salvation.

IV

God is the Supreme intelligence. God's intelligence is infinite. It can neither be reached by science that is domain-bonded, nor by reasoning that is mainly discursive. All reasoning procedures, deduction or induction, are step by step processes, from one thought to another, from known to unknown, or from principles to conclusion, and therefore can never reach the region of infinity. God's intelligence is immutable and indivisible, no succession, neither from one thought to another, nor from known to unknown, nor from principles to conclusion.

Augustine wrote, " . . . He saw that what He had made was good, when He saw that it was good to make it . . . For certainly He would not be the perfect worker He is, unless His knowledge were so perfect as to receive no addition from His finished works."

Aquinas wrote, "In the divine knowledge, there is no discursiveness. . . . God sees all things in one thing alone, which is Himself. . . . sees all things together and not successively."

Being indivisible, paradox and reason are united as a whole. Being immutable, chaos and orderliness are also united as a whole. Being immutable and indivisible, His intelligence is perfect, no paradox, nor reason, nor chaos, nor orderliness. When they are as a whole, there is perfection. When they are separated, there is imperfection. Wherever there is order, the chaos is right beside it. Wherever there is reason, the paradox is also right beside it. Therefore, only Super Unified Theory (faith and understanding) can help us to accept and understand the intuitive knowledge (axioms and principles), to accept and understand the intuitive methodologies (inductive leap, analogy, example in kinds, and color complementary rules), and to accept and understand the utmost truth — the existence of our Almighty God.

Today, human race has attained unlimited degrees of freedom, but it is still finite. The human race has also reached unbounded intelligence, but it is still finite. All these achievements are godsend gifts. God created them for us, and God allows us to attain them. All of our wisdom comes from God. It is a sin, which cannot be forgiven, to think that our wisdom is our own achievements.

Kant wrote, "My reasoning can arrive at no definite conception of the Supreme cause — which is only to be found in that of an intelligence in every respect infinite, that is, in the conception of a Deity — or establish a basis for theology."

These stiff-necked scientists shall worship God instead of worshipping an artificial methodology, the scientific method. The scientific method is valid only in the finite regions. By worshipping scientific methodology, many stiff-necked scientists are trying to elevate themselves to God's level. This notion is not only stupid but also sinful. These stiff-necked scientists can never invent or discover anything if God has not yet invented it already.

Plotinus wrote, "From the intellectual Principle, Soul is intellective, but with an intellectual operation by the method of reasonings: for its perfecting it must look to that Divine Mind, which may be thought of as a father watching over the development of his child born imperfect in comparison with himself."

In fact, all intelligences flow out from God. The evolution process, a Godsend gift, is the only way for all lives to acquire the intelligence.

V

God is the Supreme love. Tolstoy wrote, "I, with my petty understanding, begin to see clearly why she had to die, and in what way that death was but an expression of the infinite goodness of the Creator, whose every action, though generally incomprehensible to us, is but a manifestation of His infinite love for His creature."

We are His creatures. We are permanently confined in Him. We flow out from Him, will definitely return to Him. Because of His love, He has provided everything for us.

"Therefore I say unto you; Take no thought for your life, what ye shall eat, or what ye shall drink; nor yet for your body, what ye shall put on. Is not the life more than meat, and the body than raiment? Behold the fowls of the air: for they sow not, neither do they reap, nor gather into barns; yet your heavenly Father feedeth them. Are ye not much better than they?" St. Matthew 6:25-26.

Also because of His love, He has given us personal salvation.

"Not purloining, but shewing all good fidelity; that they may adorn the doctrine of God our Saviour in all things. For the grace of God that bringeth salvation hath appeared to all men." Titus 2:10-11.

Love is better than wine. Love is better than gold. We all desperately hunger for love. We want to be loved. We want to give our love. We love our spouse deeply, far deeper than the sexual love making. We love our parents for returning the love they give unto us. We love our children because we love them. We love strangers. We love animals. We love nature and all things. We love because we have unlimited love in our heart. God sowed the seed of love in our heart.

Plotinus wrote, "That our good is There is shown by the very love inborn with the soul; hence the constant linking of the Love-God with the Psyches in story and picture; the soul, other than God but sprung of Him, must needs love."

Bacon wrote, "For so we see, aspiring to be like God in power, the angels transgressed and fell; by aspiring to be like God in knowledge, man transgressed and fell; but by aspiring to a similitude of God in goodness or love, neither man nor angel ever transgressed, or shall transgress."

VI

God is the Supreme Righteousness. God creates and destroys. God did not create right and wrong; we do. God does not care one way or another how we recognize Him, through Confucianism, Taoism, Buddhism, Christianity, or even atheism. Our opinions will not change God in any way. In fact, all religions indeed worship the same God from different views in different cultures. But, God's laws are universal. All lives are created with the same laws whether they were born in Christian society or in Eastern culture or even in any far away planet. Because we are permanently confined in God, God does allow us to have unlimited freedom of choice, to be right or wrong, because of His confidence not fear.

"And the Lord said, Behold, the people is one, and they have all one language; and this they begin to do: and now nothing will be restrained from them, which they have imagined to do. Go to, let us go down, and there confound their language, that they may not understand one another's speech. So the Lord scattered them abroad from thence upon the face of all the earth: and they left off to build the city. Therefore is the name of it called Babel; because the Lord did there confound the language of all the earth: and from thence did the Lord scatter them abroad upon the face of all the earth." Genesis 11:6-9.

But, we do have to account for our own choice, to be right or wrong. The righteousness will attain awards. The wrongfulness will surely receive retribution. Award and retribution are God's law. Your action is automatically judged by the reaction; this is a generalized Newton's third law. Lawyers, judges and juries can set you free from your crime on earth, but your sin can never escape the Supreme honorable judgement from God. God is the Supreme law. The physics laws and the laws of different cultures are subsets of God's law. Scientists shall worship God if they want to understand the Supreme truth. Lawyers and judges shall worship God if they want the true justice to prevail. All citizens in the universe shall worship God if they want to attain the award and to avoid the retribution.

"A man of great wrath shall suffer punishment: for if thou deliver him, yet thou must do it again." Proverbs 19:19.

"And I saw an angel come down from heaven, having the key of the bottomless pit and a great chain in his hand. And he laid hold on the dragon, that old serpent, which is the Devil, and Satan, and bound him a thousand years." Revelation 20:1-2.

VII

God is the Supreme Self; no Being made Him. God is the Supreme Creator; everything flows out from Him. God is the Supreme Love; all loves originate from Him. God is the Supreme Intelligence; all wisdoms are given by Him. God is the Supreme Righteousness; all justices prevail in front of Him. God is paradoxicalness; the rationalism is unable to understand Him. God is chaos; the traditional science is unable to reach Him. God is nothingness; but, everything flows out from Him. The fallacy of traditional science is instinctive. The Super Unified Theory is the Theory of Everything. The Super Unified Theory is the only Way and Path to understand God because its building blocks are God Himself. I understand, therefore I worship. If you don't understand, you should worship God with faith. Confucianism, Taoism, Buddhism, and Christianity, which worship the same God with different views in different cultures, do provide a wonderful connection between God and you. The religious freedom is not a human invention but a gift from God. God is the one and the many. The one and the only God has infinite manifestations.

Book of Ethics

Ten commandments

God created universe, lives, physics laws and everything else. God's law governs the award and retribution. Nothing in the material world can last forever without changes. The physics laws will change according to the evolution stages of the universe. The civil law will change when the cultures evolve. But, God's law will never change. These ten commandments remain valid from the beginning of creation to eternity. These ten commandments are valid through out the entire universe, all cultures and all religions. Faith without understanding is hypocrisy, is superstition. With understanding, you can worship God in your own way, Taoism, Buddhism, or Christianity.

I

One, believe in God. Actually, you have no other choice but to believe in God. God is the creator. Every bit of any existence is the testimony of God's achievement. The atheists are able to deny the existence of God because God gave them the ability of free thinking. The Satan worshippers can disbelieve in God or denounce God but can never escape from God's law.

In the Westward Journey (a Chinese classic novel), there is a stone monkey story. The stone monkey who was born by a stone that was created at the moment of the first creation had very powerful magics. This monkey disturbed both heaven and earth, and none of the Arhats (Buddhist's saints) was able to arrest him. This monkey can travel millions of miles with one somersault. Finally, God came and told the monkey that if he is able to escape from God's palm, he will be set free. The monkey saw that the size of God's palm is only a few inches long; he laughed and jumped into God's hand. With one somersault, he traveled millions of miles and landed on the foot of five mountains. He marked the middle mountain with his urine to prove that he has been there, and he returned with another somersault. He told God proudly that he traveled millions of miles and returned. God showed the monkey God's hand, and the monkey smelled his own scent, which came from God's middle finger. The monkey did not escape from God's hand, and he was finally buried by the Five Finger Mountain. The peace was returned to both heaven and earth.

This story points out an important point that you can disbelieve in God but can never escape from God's law.

"The God's law is a law from whose operation we cannot for one instant in our existence escape. A law from which we may escape is not God's law," remarked Confucius.

There is one and only one God, but God has infinite manifestation. Believe in God in the way you can relate to Him. Millions of people believe in God through Jesus Christ; go for it, be a Christian. Millions of people believe in God through Buddha; go for it, be a Buddhist. Millions of people believe in God through free thinking; go for it, be an atheist. But, the supreme way of believing in God is through a true enlightenment, by studying the Books of Truth, Faith and Life.

"God is indestructible. Being indestructible, God is eternal. Being eternal, God is self-existent. Being self-existent, God is infinite. Being infinite, God is vast and deep. Being vast and deep, God is transcendental and intelligent. It is because God is vast and deep that God contains all existence. It is because God is transcendental and intelligent that God embraces all existence. It is because God is infinite and eternal that God fulfills and perfects all existence," remarked Confucius.

II

Two, be a self. God is the Supreme Self. No Being made God, for God is the only Supreme Being. You are the image of one of God's manifestation. You are a self, a small self. Actually, you have no other choice but be yourself. You can imitate your idol with your whole life, but you can never become him. Nobody else is able to help you to be yourself. God already gave every self the intelligence, love and life. Keep this Godsend gift to develop your life and do not beg for more.

"Wherefore it is that a self must watch diligently over what his eyes cannot see and is in fear and awe of what his ears cannot hear.

"There is nothing more evident than that which cannot be seen by the eyes and nothing more palpable than that which cannot be perceived by the senses. Wherefore a self must watch diligently over his secret thoughts [You are yourself and do not deceive yourself.]

"When the passions, such as joy, anger, grief, and pleasure, have not awakened, that is our central self, or moral being. When these passions awaken and each and all attain due measure and degree, that is harmony, or the moral order. Our central self or moral being is the great basis of existence, and harmony for moral order is the universal law in the world.

"When our true central self and harmony are realized, the universe then becomes a cosmos and all things attain their full growth and development.

"Being true to oneself is the law of God. To try to be true to oneself is the law of men.

"He who is naturally true to himself is one who, without effort, hits upon what is right, and without thinking understands what he wants to know, whose life is easily and naturally in harmony with God's law," remarked Confucius.

The God's law is to be found in your "self." You can find in no situation in life in which you are not master of yourself.

III

Three, make your life meaningful. God gave you life, wisdom and will power, but it depends upon you yourself to develop its meaning. You can be a winner if you want to be a winner. You will be a loser if you want to be a loser. Once upon a time, an angel descended upon three boys. He told the first boy, "You are gifted; you will host parties for three thousand guests every day." He told the other two boys, "You can have good lives if you work hard to achieve it." These two boys worked very hard and had very successful careers. But, the gifted boy was waiting for the prediction to become true. Thirty years later, while he was begging food on the street, he met the angel again. He asked the angel with an angry screaming voice, "Where are my three thousand guests and the daily feast?" The angel answered calmly, "The three thousand fleas on your body do have banquets daily."

The Buddha said, "Even if one escapes from the evil creations, it is one's rare fortune to be born as a human being. Even if one be born as human, it is one's rare fortune to be perfect in all the six senses. Even if he be perfect in all the six senses, it is his rare fortune to see the enlightened. Even if he be able to see the enlightened, it is his rare fortune to have his heart awakened in faith. Even if he have faith, it is his rare fortune to awaken the heart of intelligence. Even if he awakens the heart of intelligence, it is his rare fortune to realize a spiritual state which is above discipline and attainment."

You are the winner at the moment your life begins. Every life begins by defeating millions of competitors; only one out of millions of sperms is able to unite with an egg.

As Buddha said, there are many levels of attainments for life. There are many winners in the world. You were a winner. It depends upon yourself to make your life meaningful.

IV

Four, love all lives and all things. God is the Supreme love. God sowed the seed of love in your heart. Actually, you have no other choice but to fall in love with someone you love. You shall not destroy or steal someone else's love. If you covet your neighbor's house and wife, you have lost your love for your neighbor. The enmities will surely grow between you and your neighbor, and you will surely receive retribution.

You shall love the unborn. Life begins at Conception. For a bisexual reproduction process, an ovarian cell that is diploid has two sets of chromosomes. This ovarian cell will become a functional egg that is haploid and contains only one set of chromosomes. The egg and sperm lost half of the genetical message after they were produced, and they are definitely not the same kind of life form as their producers. It is very clear that the first generation of life (haploid state, egg and sperm) and the second generation of life (diploid state, human life) are completely different. Neither the female's egg nor the male's sperm are able to escape the inevitable fate of death unless a unification process takes place between them. A human life, a second generation life form, is created as soon as a haploid egg and a haploid sperm are unifed. Every embryo carries all the genetic message, which a life can ever possess. There is essentially no difference between a born human and a human embryo; anyone who denies this fact is either an idiot or a liar. Many societies deny the rights of unborn; they are definitely immoral.

But, the rights of a woman to control her own body and her future and the rights of a society to control its population growth and the greater well-being of the mankind also cannot be denied. Abortion is definitely a killing. But, killing is also God's way. In God, killing is the way for creating new lives and for sustaining all lives. God created food chains to sustain your life. Love and killing seem to contradict each other, but the paradoxicalness is God's way. Killing is God's art, and you shall not imitate it. You ought to obey the laws of your culture. You ought to love all lives and all things. You are nailed down in the environment by your own gut.

V

Five, get along with others. You are a small self in a lively super organism, the mankind. You are a self but not alone. If you denounced the others, the others are not only victimized by your conduct, but they will surely fight back and hurt you. On the other hand, if you are weak-minded, you are often inviting the aggression. There are many different ways to get along with others in many different cultures.

In Christian society, follow the Christian Ten Commandments.

"Honour thy father and thy mother.

"Thou shalt not kill.

"Thou shalt not commit adultery.

"Thou shalt not steal.

"Thou shalt not bear false witness against thy neighbor.

"Thou shalt not covet thy neighbor's house, thou shalt not covet thy neighbor's wife, nor his manservant, nor his maidservant, nor his ox, nor his ass, nor any thing that is thy neighbor's." Exodus 20:12-17.

In Confucianism, Confucius said, "What you do not wish others should do unto you, do not do unto them.

"In a high position he does not domineer over his subordinates. In a subordinate position he does not court the favors of his superiors. He puts in order his own personal conduct and seeks nothing from others; hence he has no complaint to make. He complains not against God, nor rails against men.

"In the practice of archery we have something resembling the principle in a moral man's life. When the archer missed the center of the target, he turns round and seeks for the cause of his failure within himself."

In Buddhism, Buddha said, "Evil doers who denounce the wise resemble a person who spits against the sky; the spittle will never reach the sky, but comes down on himself.

"There are ten things considered good by all beings, and ten things evil. What are they? Three of them depend upon the body, four upon the mouth, and three upon thought.

"Three evil deeds depending upon the body are: killing, stealing, and committing adultery. The four depending upon the mouth are: slandering, cursing, lying, and flattery. The three depending upon thought are: envy, anger, and infatuation. All these things are against the Holy Way, and therefore they are evil.

"When these evils are not done, there are ten good deeds."

You shall follow the rules of your own culture for getting along with others. Also, each culture shall respect one another. The discrimination among cultures and races is most evil. Even King Solomon was a victim of the color discrimination.

"I am black, but comely, O ye daughters of Jerusalem, as the tents of Kedar, as the curtains of Solomon. Look not upon me, because I am black, because the sun hath looked upon me: my mother's children were angry with me; they made me the keeper of the vineyards; but mine own vineyard have I not kept." Solomon's Song 1:5-6.

We are part of one super organism, and there is no way to change that; therefore, we shall get along with one another.

VI

Six, dwell in truth and perfection. The bare testimonies and the revelation of God is self-evident and understandable. We all are able to understand this utmost truth with the unification of three priniples, reasoning (self-evidence principle), science (hypotheses principle), and faith (religions). This three is one. With all three, we can attain the truth and the perfection. With any "one" alone, we can only grasp a limited truth. With any "two" combinations, we are still unable to reach the utmost truth and perfection. The truth is eternal. The truth is infinity. The truth is immutable. The truth is indivisible. Because it is indivisible, infinite limited truths can be created by it. See Book of Truth (IV) and Book of Life (III).

Augustine wrote, "Thus when one man says to me: 'Moses meant what I think,' and another 'Not at all, he meant what I think,' it seems to me that the truly religious thing is to say: Why should he not have meant both, if both are true; and if in the same words some should see a third and a fourth meaning and any other number of true meanings, why should we not believe that Moses saw them all, since by him one God tempered Sacred Scripture to the minds of many who should see truths in it, yet not all the same truths."

Indeed, the one is the many, and the many is the one. God resides in the universe; the entire universe resides in God.

Aristotle wrote, "All contraries are reducible to being and non-being and to unity and plurality, as for instance, rest belongs to unity and movement to plurality . . . And everything else is evidently reducible to unity and plurality. . . . For all things are either contraries or composed of contraries, and unity and plurality are the principles of all contrariety."

With this understanding, we shall and can dwell in truth and perfection. The greatness of Confucius, Buddha, Jesus Christ, and even the greatness of many stiff-necked scientists have enabled us to understand this utmost truth. We shall dwell in their greatness. But if you are unable to reach this understanding, then the way of striving for perfection is by doing little things well. As a son, be the best son. As a father, be the best father. As a husband or a wife, be the best husband or the best wife.

VII

Seven, attain your faith and salvation with understanding, works, ceremonies, and prayers. Faith without understanding is hypocrisy, is superstition. It is also impossible for anyone to attain an instant salvation without works. Anyone who is trying to sell you an instant salvation is either a stupid liar or an evil liar.

"Even so faith, if it hath not works, is dead, being alone. Yea, a man may say, Thou hast faith, and I have works: shew me thy faith without thy works, and I will shew thee my faith by my works. Thou believest that there is one God; thou doest well: the devils also believe, and tremble. But wilt thou know, O vain man, that faith without works is dead? Was not Abraham our father justified by works, when he had offered Isaac his son upon the altar? Seest thou how faith wrought with his works, and by works was faith made perfect?

"Ye see then how that by works a man is justified, and not by faith only.

"For as the body without the spirit is dead, so faith without works is dead also." James 2:17-26.

The works is the only factor that will be used on the judgement. "And I saw the dead, small and great, stand before God; and the books were opened: and another book was opened, which is the book of life: and the dead were judged out of those things which were written in the books, according to their works. And the sea gave up the dead which were in it; and death and hell delivered up the dead which were in them: and they were judged every man according to their works." Revelation 20:12-13.

There is no way you can attain faith without work just the same as you cannot become a scholar without study. You cannot become a Christian if you do not go to a church, neither study Bible, nor obey Christian moral codes. How can anyone have a faith and know the truth if he has not yet set out to search for one?

Lin Yutang, a sincere Christian, wrote, "I am sure there are many Christians who never made this quest; they found the Christian God when they were in the cradle, and, like the wife of Abraham, they took this God with them wherever they went; and finally, when they reached the grave, the same God was with them still. Religion of this kind is like a piece of furniture or a possession that you can tuck away and take along in your journey wherever you go, . . . I believe that many churches prefer to sell religion in a package. It is compact, and so much more convenient to carry around. That is a comfortable and easy way to come by religion. I doubt, however, the value of religion of this sort."

Buddha also said, "If a man who has committed many a misdemeanor does not repent and cleanse his heart of the evil, retribution will come upon his person as sure as the streams run into the ocean which becomes ever deeper and wider.

"If a man who has committed a misdemeanor come to the knowledge of it, reform himself, and practise goodness, the force of retribution will gradually exhaust itself as a disease gradually loses its baneful influence when the patient perspires."

Furthermore, all works shall be done with sincerity. Only sincere-will can attain honorable works. Only by setting your mind right, the sincere-will can be attained. Only by praying to God, you are able to set your mind right.

Confucius said, "When your mind is not there, you look but do not see, listen but do not hear and eat but do not know the flavor of the food."

You shall set your mind sincere and pray to God daily. Ku Hung-ming wrote, "The true Christian is one who is a Christian because 'it is his nature to be so,' because he loves holiness and all that is lovable in Christianity. . . . That is the true Christian. The sneak Christian is one who wants to be a Christian because he is afraid of hell-fire. The cad Christian is one who wants to be a Christian because he wishes to go to Heaven to drink tea and sing hymns with the angels."

The whole universe resides in God, but God also resides in you. Scientists can never understand this simple fact because the traditional science does not have a method to find out the supreme truth. Scientists exclude God from their work; therefore, God excludes them from knowing the real truth. With prayer, you can attain the truth as God is the only supreme truth. You may not know physics, mathematics and other sciences, but you do know the supreme truth if you believe in God and pray to God. Satan has faith but no work. Faith without work is Satanic faith. Faith without understanding is the faith of a liar.

VIII

Eight, respect all religions. Summer bugs never know about winter snow because they can never live past autumn. It is not their fault to be ignorant; it is their lives. But, it is indeed very frustrating to hear that summer bugs deny the existence of the winter snow. To be ignorant is okay, but to denounce others because of the ignorance is annoying. Many people denounce other people's religion, either pagan or Christianity, while they have no slightest idea about what the other religions are. How can anyone disdain other's belief while he doesn't know what he is denouncing about? Nonetheless, this ignorance can be forgiven and should be forgiven. The one who knows shall forgive the one who does not. Nonetheless, the act or thought of one religion to denounce another is indeed evil.

In fact, all religions have the same structure if their superficial difference is peeled off. All religions are constructed with identical architecture but with different kinds of exterior decorations. They all have four corner stones: 1) A Creator. 2) A method of connection and attainment. 3) A method of manifestation—miracles. 4) A set of ethic codes for earth life.

Therefore, all religions are virtually equal. This notion is even written in the Christian Bible.

"Now there are diversities of gifts, but the same Spirit. And there are differences of administrations, but the same Lord. And there are diversities of operations, but it is the same God which worketh all in all. But the manifestation of the Spirit is given to every man to profit withal. For to one is given by the Spirit the word of wisdom; to another the word of knowledge by the same Spirit; To another faith by the same Spirit; to another the gifts of healing by the same Spirit; To another the working of miracles; to another prophecy; to another discerning of spirits; to another divers kinds of tongues; to another the intepretation of tongues:" 1 Corinthians 12:4-10.

Some of the religions are more popular because they promise a free ticket for all sinners to go straight to heaven regardless of what kind of evil deeds they have done. There is no right or wrong value for this kind of promise; it is outside the domain of the truth. Actually, no religion has ever touched the domain of the truth. The Buddhism and the original Taoism have tried to reach the domain of truth but have failed. The following quotations are the highest understanding of their search.

Buddha said, "The Way is beyond words and expressions, is bound by nothing earthly. Lose sight of it to an inch, or miss it for a moment, and we are away from it forevermore."

Lao-tze said, "The Tao that can be spoken is not the Eternal Tao. The name that can be named is not the Eternal name. Nameless, the Tao is the Source of Heaven and Earth; Named, it is the Mother of all beings."

In the legend of the Tower of Tongues, Temple of the Seven Lights of the Earth, all cultures came from one race and one culture. Today, we have different languages and different religions. The differences among religions do evolve into different cultures. Now is the time to unify all religions again through respecting all religions.

IX

Nine, worship God through fellowship. You are a self but not alone. You shall love others. You shall get along with others. You shall make your life meaningful for yourself and for others. You shall believe in God by yourself and with others. You shall respect the different opinions and cultures of others. You shall worship God with others.

"For the body is not one member, but many. If the foot shall say, Because I am not the hand, I am not of the body; is it therefore not of the body? And if the ear shall say, Because I am not the eye, I am not of the body; is it therefore not of the body? If the whole body were an eye, where were the hearing? If the whole were hearing, where were the smelling? But now hath God set the members every one of them in the body, as it hath pleased him. And if they were all one member, where were the body? But now are they many members, yet but one body. And the eye cannot say unto the hand, I have no need of thee: nor again the head to feet, I have no need of you. Nay, much more those members of the body, which seem to be more feeble, are necessary: And those members of the body, which we think to be less honourable, upon these we bestow more abundant honour; and our uncomely parts have more abundant comeliness. For our comely parts have no need: but God hath tempered the body together, having given more abundant honour to that part which lacked: That there should be no schism in the body; but that the members should have the same care one for another. And whether one member suffer, all the members suffer with it; or one member be honoured, all the members rejoice with it." 1 Corinthians 12:14-26.

Again, we shall not discriminate other races and cultures because we all are part of one body. We shall worship God through fellowship and establish a unified church.

X

Ten, eliminate all nuclear arms. The only way to rescue our civilization from a nuclear holocaust is to eliminate all nuclear arms.

The nuclear deterrent has successfully prevented nuclear war for decades. The concept of the nuclear deterrent is developed under an assumption that nuclear war cannot be won and a meaningful retaliation is able to be launched under a full-scale preemptive nuclear strike. Therefore, the nuclear deterrent will remain as peacekeeper to prevent nuclear war. This logic is invalid for two reasons.

First, any meaningful retaliation which can be launched under a full-scale preemptive nuclear strike is impossible. For the reason of preventing accidental or unauthorized use of nuclear weapons, a negative control system is implemented in all kinds of nuclear command system. The negative control makes it impossible for any individual to fire nuclear weapons and improbable that the necessary combination of people could be organized in the absence of plausible political authority. Therefore, all warheads become useless when the negative control cannot be unlocked. When the nuclear arsenal increases, a stronger and more rigid negative control is needed, and the chance of unlocking this rigid negative control is almost nil under a full-scale preemptive nuclear strike. Launch under attack is impractical and impossible. With nuclear weapons on hand, a nuclear holocaust is inevitable.

Second, God does allow mad men to exist. Not only a mad man can become a leader of a country which does possess nuclear arsenal, but a mad man can produce some nuclear weapons without great difficulty. Furthermore, it is immoral to punish a small country for developing nuclear arsenal while some countries are stock piling nuclear warheads. It is not God's law to demand the elimination of nuclear weapons, but it is God's law to eliminate all immoral behaviors. No super power is able to oppress a small nation forever. During the 6000 years of known history, no nation is able to be a super power forever. There is no way to prevent small countries to acquire some nuclear weapons, and the nuclear holocaust is inevitable.

God created the universe, lives and civilization. God does demand that all and all return to Him. With nuclear arsenal on earth, we will surely destroy the civilization before the judgement day. The only way to rescue our civilization from a nuclear holocaust is to eliminate all nuclear arms.

Book of Truth (VI)

Super Unification

Thy kingdom come, Thy will be done. God created the universe, lives and everything else. God demands that all things and all beings return to Him; there is no other choice. So, both you and I know the final answer — our universe will crunch into a big fire ball, then this fire ball will incarnate into a new universe that is constructed with anti-matter.

But, how exactly does this crunch process work? What is the fuel of the fire ball? How does this fire ball retain the genetic message for all lives that will surely reappear in the next universe?

II

When we burn coals, the fire contains carbon particles. At the big crunch, the fire ball contains prequarks only. The steps of decomposing process that decomposes elementary particles (protons, neutrons, leptons and quarks) to prequark (the most basic building block created by God) can be reversed to construct a new set of elementary particles.

At here, I will show you how all elementary particles are made. God created everything from nothing. In fact, God only makes two kinds of building blocks, Vacutron and Angultron; everything is constructed with these two prequarks.

Vacutron is a vacuum or nothing; it does not carry electric charge and mass.

Angultron is a trisected angle. It carries 1/3 units of electric charge. It is the building block for constructing space. It also carries mass. With Angultron, mass, space, time and electric charge appear. Why are both space and time trisected (divided by 3), neither by 2, nor by any other number? Because, for any given angle, only trisecting process requires infinite steps, by using a compass and a straight edge that are the only two tools existing in nature naturally. And, the creation process of Angulton has to be an infinte to finite transformation, the only process capable of transferring "Nothing" to "Something." See my book, Super Unifed Theory, for details.

Angultron trisects space. It means that each space is subdivided into three seats. For each seat, it can be either empty (Vacutron) or occupied (Angultron). Therefore, only four different kind of particles can be formed:

1) A particle with all seats which are occupied by Angultrons carries one unit of electric charge, and it is named electron or lepton.

2) A particle with two seats which are occupied by Angultrons carries ⅔ units of electric charge, and it is named UP quark.

3) A particle with only one seat which is occupied by Angultron carries ⅓ units of electric charge, and it is named DOWN quark.

4) A particle with no seat which is occupied by Angultron carries zero unit of electric charge, and it is named neutrino or lepton.

Furthermore, for a given quark, there are three ways to arrange the seating, and each seating is distinguishable from others. Physicists have chosen three color labels to identify these differences. So, two quarks (UP and DOWN) evolve into six distinguishable quarks. In fact, the entire universe is constructed with these eight elementary particles (six quarks and two leptons), and their structure can be represented with the following formulas.

Electron is (A, A, A1)   A is Angultron
Neutrino is (V, V, V1)   V is Vacutron

For quarks, there are three varieties for each quark, and they are identified with three color labels, red, yellow and blue.

	Red	Yellow	Blue
UP quark	(V, A, A1)	(A, V, A1)	(A, A, V1)
DOWN quark	−(A, V, V1)	−(V, A, V1)	−(V, V, A1)

Two notions shall be mentioned here. First, the quark color corresponds to a special seating arrangement. I have chosen the first seat to be red, yellow for the second seat, blue for the third. The quark color is identified by the seat's color which is occupied by a minority prequark. For example, V is the minority prequark in (V, A, A1), and it seats on the red seat; so, (V, A, A1) has red color. Second, there is a number 1 attached on the third seat. Not only space is trisected, time is also trisected. The life time of the universe is divided into three stages, and they are represented by three generations of quarks. These three generations are indentified with three numbers, 1, 2 and 3. They are attached on the third seat.

III

The reason for this universe to be stable and alive is because proton is stable and alive. But, God demands that all things and all beings return to Him; so, protons must die at the point of big crunch. So far, all proton decay experiments around the world have failed to observe any proton decay case.

Proton can never die at this stage of the universe for the same reason as you could never breathe before you were conceived; you do breathe now. Proton will die under the proper condition, second or third generation stages.

Today, the entire universe is constructed with eight elementary particles, two leptons and six quarks. But, the lifetime of the universe has three phases; therefore, twenty-four elementary particles are needed to represent them all. Again, the only reason for the existence of these two additional generations of elementary particles is to provide a process to kill the proton or to create it.

Physicists gave those quarks and leptons some funny names, such as UP, Down, Charm, etc.; you should not be confused by these funny names; they are just labels.

The second and third generation elementary particles have the same structure as the first ones but with different mass and generation numbers. Their structure and formula are listed below.

The following is the formula for second generation elementary particles:

Muon is $-(A, A, A2)$

There are also two leptons, muon and muon neutrino.

Muon neutrino is $(V, V, V2)$

There are two quarks, Charm and Strange.

	Red	Yellow	Blue
Charm quark	$(V, A, A2)$	$(A, V, A2)$	$(A, A, V2)$
Strange quark	$-(A, V, V2)$	$-(V, A, V2)$	$-(V, V, A2)$

The following is the formula for third generation elementary particles:

There are two leptons, tau and tau neutrino.

Tau is $\quad -(A, A, A3)$

Tau neutrino is $(V, V, V3)$

There are also two quarks, Top and Bottom.

	Red	Yellow	Blue
Top quark	(V, A, A3)	(A, V, A3)	(A, A, V3)
Bottom quark	−(A, V, V3)	−(V, A, V3)	−(V, V, A3)

IV

Now, we are able to describe the death process of a proton. Proton is composed by two UP quarks (with different quark colors) and one DOWN quark. Proton has one unit of electrical charge, and it is colorless. So, all quark colors have to cancel out with one another. Indeed, they do. The following diagram describes one of the proton structures.

Proton (colorless, one unit of electric charge)
Blue UP quark   (A, A, V1)   third seat color shows up.
Red UP quark   (V, A, A1)   first seat color shows up.
Anti-yellow Down quark   −(V, A, V1)   second seat color shows up.

Very clearly, this structure produces one unit of positive electrical charge (4 positive Angultrons and one negative one). It also produces a colorless proton; blue and red form a complimentary yellow which cancels out with anti-yellow. This is a very stable structure for both attributes, colors and electric charge.

The only way to destroy proton is by unbalancing either color balance or electric stability. The following diagram describes one of the options.

The Angultron which seated at the third seat of the Red UP quark moves to the third seat of Blue UP quark. This single movement results the creation of a positron (colorless) and a yellow anti-Down quark.

Colorless positron   (A, A, A1)
Yellow anti-Down quark   (V, A, V1) second seat color
Anti-yellow Down quark   −(V, A, V1) second seat color

Again, both electric charge and quark colors are balanced. One and only one movement is needed to complete this process, moving one Angultron from Red UP quark to the empty seat of the Blue UP quark. But, this single movement process cannot take place until it is imbedded in a very high energy reservoir that has an equivalent energy density the same as the one was at the big bang. In other words, the protons will die when our universe collapses.

V

Our universe will definitely collapse because of the existence of the ghost partner. This is the necessary consequence of the creation process, from nothing to something. It is absolutely necessary to pay back the something that was borrowed. The chance for science to prove this fact is nil because it is beyond the reach of science. But, this ghost partner is visualized in the form as a unified force that can be described with the following formula.

The unifed force (F) is equal to a "coupling factor (K)" times the "Plank's constant (h)" then divided by "the effected space (dS)" times "the duration of the time (dT)."

$$F \text{ (unifed)} = Kh/(dS*dT)$$

With this equation, we are able to derive the Heisenberg's uncertainty principle. This principle says that if we want to locate an object, then we have to throw something (a signal) to hit the object then analyze the returned signal, such as the echo location method used by bats. However, there is a problem for this method. For example, if the signal that we throw out is a golf ball and the object that we try to detect is also a golf ball, then this object ball will be knocked to move to a new location when it was hit by the signal ball. So, the old location that was identified by the signal ball is no longer the actual location of the object ball. The old location of the object ball is a false answer for our quest because the object ball has moved to a new location. In other words, at this situation, all the answers we can get is the history, not the true answer of the present. In fact, no one is able to find out the exact location of the object ball by using a signal ball that has an approximate same mass. On the other hand, if we use a small green bean to detect a big basketball, then we can always get an accurate answer because the small green bean is unable to relocate the big ball.

In general, we use light or sound to detect the location of an object. For most of the visible objects, they are much heavier than the signal ball, light or sound wave. Therefore, the location of the object will not be altered by the impact of the signal ball. So, we are able to locate these objects with a precise accuracy. In the micro-world, if the mass of the signal ball is in the same order as the object ball, then we will not be able to locate the object of this micro-world as easy as what we can do in the marco-world. This phenomenon is called Heisenberg's uncertainty principle and can be represented with the following formula.

The momentum change (dP) times the location change (dS) is always larger than the Plank's constant.

dP * ds > = h

For most people, this formula does not mean much. Actually, this formula can be understood easily with common language. If we want to detect the location of an object very accurately, it means that dS approaches to zero, then the direction (dP) of this object where it is going cannot be determined (dP approaches to infinity). On the other hand, if we want to know exactly where it is going (dP → 0), then the location (dS) of this object cannot be determined (dS approaches to infinity).

So far, the Heisenberg's uncertainty principle is not a fundamental law but correct only in the domain of the micro-world. It is the foundational principle of the entire quantum mechanics that describes the governing laws of electron, proton, neutron and many other elementary particles.

Very obviously, this uncertainty principle is not wrong, but all physicists have misunderstood it. It is not only accurate in the micro-world, but also the origin of chaos of the marco-world. A new uncertainty principle can be derived with unified force equation very easily.

In physics, the momenta change (dP) is equal to force (F) times the duration (dT) of the force.

dP = F (unified) * dT

So, dP * dS = F * dT * dS

= (Kh/(dT * dS)) * (dT * dS)

= Kh

The Heisenberg's uncertainty principle is dP * dS > = h. Obviously, the old formula is a subset of the new formula. When K (coupling constant) is larger than or equal to 1, then dP * dS is larger than or equal to h (Plank's constant); this is the old formula that describes the micro-world. When K is very small, such as the gravitation coupling, then Kh is approaching to zero; therefore, both location and direction of an object can be measured very accurately.

VI

It is a miracle that both the micro and the macro world can be described with a single equation. This is the dream which Einstein devoted his life time for but failed to make it become true. He spent all of his life trying to unify the electric force and the gravitational force but failed. Surprisingly, the unification of these two forces is amazingly simple.

The electric charge is carried by Angultron that is manifested from the division of the space. The Plank constant is the unit of space. The smallest space is one Plank constant; therefore, the electric charge has also to be measured by Plank constant. Actually, one electric charge is equal to the square root of one-half Plank constant times light speed. The light speed (C) is the fastest speed a signal can be transmitted in the finite world. Nevertheless, signals can be transmitted faster than light speed in the infinite state that exists in both big bang and big crunch.

So, one unit of charge = square root of ($\frac{1}{2}$ * h * C)

The electric force between two charges is equal to charge one (q1) times charge two (q2) divided by the square of the distance (r square) between these two charges.

F (electric) = q1 * q2/r square

        = mq * nq/r square

        = m(square root of $\frac{1}{2}$*h*C) * n(square root of $\frac{1}{2}$*h*C)/r square

        = ($\frac{1}{2}$ * m * n)(h * C)/r square

        = f1 (h * C/r square) . . . Equation 1

The f1 is the coupling constant for electric force.

The gravitational force between two masses is equal to mass one (m1) times mass two (m2) times the gravitational constant (G) divided by the square of the distance (r square) between these two masses. At here, G (gravitational constant) is equal to Plank constant times light speed divided by x square.

G = h * C/ x square

The "x" is the mass unit that is determined by the time unit (quanta) with the following formula.

x = h/(time unit * C square)

At the beginning of the creation, the time unit was a quanta, which is a lot larger than today's time unit that seems to be a continuous wave; so the mass unit was a lot smaller then. Therefore, the gravitational constant was a lot larger or stronger at the beginning of the creation than what it is today. This is why all those old galaxies can be held together with a lot less mass than today's Newton law allows. Today, many scientists are trying to find the so called dark matter that is the invisible mass for those old galaxies but all have failed.

$$
\begin{aligned}
F \text{ (gravitational)} &= G * m1 * m2/r \text{ square} \\
&= (h * C/x \text{ square})(m1 * m2)/r \text{ square} \\
&= (m1 * m2/x \text{ square})(h * C/r \text{ square}) \\
&= f2 \ (h * C/r \text{ square}) \ \ldots \ \text{Equation 2}
\end{aligned}
$$

The f2 is the coupling constant for gravitational force.

In fact, the only difference betweeen the Equation 1 and Equation 2 is that they have two different coupling constants, and both of them have the same structure as the unified force does. The r square can be written as dS * dS = dS * dT * C.

$$
\begin{aligned}
\text{So, } F \text{ (gravitational)} &= f2 \ (h * C/(dS * dT * C)) \\
&= f2 * h/(dS * dT)
\end{aligned}
$$

This is the unified force formula. The electric force also can be written in this form with the same procedure.

VII

I have not only unified all forces, but used only very simple algebra that can be understood by every eighth grade student. After you read this book, you already know more truth than all physicists do. Furthermore, the unification of all forces has a very important significance. There is one and only one God who is manifested as the unified force. This unified force will then further manifest into many other forces, physical, mental and social forces. The fallacy of traditional science is fundamentally profound. Not only the methodology of traditional science is very much unsound, but it also does not have any philosophical foundation. The unlimited success of science in the domain of finite world is as a peanut, compared with the success of religions, because it is unable to reach the single utmost truth, the existence of God. There are many, many untrue stories in all religions, but the single truth that was recognized by them has made them great cultures.

Pdf of books & URLs

Nature's Manifesto:
https://tienzengong.files.wordpress.com/20
17/12/4th-natures-manifesto.pdf

PreBabel – the universal and perfect
language:
https://tienzengong.files.wordpress.com/20
20/04/2nd-prebabel-the-universal.pdf

Bible of China Studies:
https://tienzengong.files.wordpress.com/20
18/03/bible-of-china-studies.pdf

This is a book about religion and logic that will twist the reader's brain in delightfully new and different ways of thinking. The author provokes his reader to think, not only through his unique logic but also via his inventive language and tongue-in-cheek chiding of people who are locked into traditional thought patterns. Gong attempts to unify seeming opposites: science and religion, finite and infinity, singularity and totality, religion and religions, reasoning and faith. His Theory of Everything, which is ironically the Theory of Nothing, might be called a "Unification Theory."

The book is timely in its introduction of a foundation for a "New Theology" and in its explanation of how religions guide and direct our energies to influence the development of our societies. The book is welcome because it does not contradict any religion but instead affirms all faiths, the truths underlying all religions, the truth of mathematics and science.

It is perhaps a book that could be written only by someone such as Gong, for it uniquely blends, encompasses and transcends Oriental and Western science, math and religion.

Dolly Maley Tarver
Associate Professor of English